C000003081

Crowning the Year

Crowning the Year

Liturgy, theology and ecclesiology for the rural church

Tom Clammer OC

CANTERBURY
PRESS
Norwich

© Tom Clammer OC 2021

Published in 2021 by Canterbury Press
Editorial office
3rd Floor, Invicta House,
108–114 Golden Lane,
London EC1Y 0TG, UK
www.canterburypress.co.uk

Canterbury Press is an imprint of Hymns Ancient & Modern Ltd
(a registered charity)

Hymns Ancient & Modern® is a registered trademark of
Hymns Ancient & Modern Ltd
13A Hellesdon Park Road, Norwich,
Norfolk NR6 5DR, UK

All rights reserved. No part of this publication may be reproduced,
stored in a retrieval system, or transmitted,
in any form or by any means, electronic, mechanical,
photocopying or otherwise, without the prior permission of
the publisher, Canterbury Press.

The Author has asserted his right under the Copyright, Designs and
Patents Act 1988 to be identified as the Author of this Work.

Scripture quotations are from New Revised Standard Version Bible:
Anglicized Edition, copyright © 1989, 1995 National Council of
the Churches of Christ in the United States of America. Used by
permission. All rights reserved worldwide.

British Library Cataloguing in Publication data

A catalogue record for this book is available
from the British Library

978-1-78622-339-5

Typeset by Regent Typesetting
Printed and bound by
CPI Group (UK) Ltd

For the people of the Severnside Benefice
and the
Parish of Tidenham.
Thank you for teaching me to pray.

Contents

Acknowledgements

This book is really a set of collective thoughts arising from 25 years of praying in the countryside. My chief thanks go to the people who formed me in those contexts, who taught me to pray, who prayed with me when I was tempted to give up, and with whom I pray today. It is for these reasons I dedicate this book to the people of the Severnside Benefice and the Parish of Tidenham. Those are the places where the ideas I explore here were formed. They are the people who taught me how buildings, places and communities really are filled with angels and join in heaven's song. By name I thank Brian Green, Royston Grosvenor and David Treharne: my own incumbents in Tidenham, and Kay Mundy, Charles Whitney, Tom Curtis and Carolyn Methven, for so many shared times of prayer.

The present incumbents of Tidenham and Severnside, David Treharne and Ilse Ferwerde, have been generous in reading sections of this book that specifically concern their parishes, giving permission for their inclusion and offering insight.

I thank Christine and the team at Canterbury Press for believing there are things of value in this book and for their encouragement and patience during the writing process.

Sarah Flanaghan proofread the entire text, which in itself is a sacrifice worthy of much thanksgiving.

The Gloucestershire Echo and Corinna Pippard both provided several of the photographs contained within the book and gave their permission for their publication.

I hope this book ties together two of the chief loves of my life: geography and practical theology. That I am a liturgist is thanks to the late Michael Perham, who ordained me and licensed me to my rural incumbency. That I am a geographer is chiefly down to my father, Richard Clammer, who instilled a deep love of the exploration of people and place long ago. For that, and for the beautiful maps which offer such a lively and human insight into the places that I love, thanks Dad! To be able to refer in the bibliography to my mum's lovely work on the churches of Tidenham Parish makes my book a delightfully family affair in a year in which we have been otherwise physically separated.

As ever, so many thanks to my patient and long-suffering wife Emma, for not only navigating being married to a rural incumbent with such poise, grace and love, but for once again being willing to humour me through the experience of producing a book.

List of Abbreviations

TFC	A Time for Creation
ASB	Alternative Service Book 1980
BCP	The Book of Common Prayer 1662
CW	Common Worship: Services and Prayers for the Church of England
CW: DP	Common Worship: Daily Prayer
CW: OS	Common Worship: Ordination Services Study Edition
CW: PS	Common Worship: Pastoral Services
CW: TS	Common Worship: Times and Seasons
LHWE	Lent, Holy Week and Easter
NEH	New English Hymnal
NPW	New Patterns for Worship
PHG	The Promise of His Glory

List of Illustrations

Foreword

by the Rt Revd Sarah Mullally

When I asked Tom why he wanted the Bishop of London to write a foreword for his book he suggested that I would bring really useful insights because I have been a suffragan in a deeply rural diocese and am now rooted in a very urban centre. He believed that I would be able to speak to the ecclesiological 'stuff' he was addressing with an authority that would be very useful. Well, I enjoy writing about 'stuff' and I submit this as a foreword to a book which I feel offers much insight to the rural church.

I feel very privileged to have been a suffragan Bishop in the Diocese of Exeter. As the Bishop of Crediton I learnt of the importance of place; I saw how all ministry is done in context; and the people were a joy.

I have sat for the last few years as co-chair for the All-Party Parliamentary Group on Rural Health, maybe for the same reason I am writing this foreword, in that I know the difference between the rural and the urban and how their context shapes the lives of those who live there. On leaving Devon I was left with the deep impression of the isolation of rural communities: isolation from public services, isolation from schools and isolation from people. Which means you can't look at health services in the rural setting as you do in the city, in the same way that you can't look at the rural church in the same way as the urban church.

The nature and distinctiveness of rural communion means that the rural church is not a failed urban one but one that is part of the Body of Christ, offering much to the benefit of the whole as we grow in maturity under Christ as our head.

Travelling to churches in deeply rural parts of Devon I could not help but see how there was a relationship between place and a worshipping community. My first Advent Sunday in Devon I changed in a small church vestry in freezing temperatures with the sound of cattle the other side of the stained glass windows, and the church was full. The worship was no less special than the Darkness to Light Services at Salisbury Cathedral attended by thousands at which I was present the previous year – both told the story of God's love.

A mainstay of my ministry in Devon was the blessing of bells, towers, stained glass windows and even a gargoyle. Buildings are, as Tom suggests, sacraments in stone. Rural church buildings speak of God in the same way as cathedrals. In rural villages people feel a strong sense of connection to their church building: it not only speaks of God but of their history and their future. There in their buildings they continue to celebrate the liturgical seasons as people of 'The Way'.

God starts where people are, and I saw church communities in Devon becoming confident about their strengths and honest about their weaknesses and the reality of their need for others. Churches often work together to bring about positive change for the whole community. Like the Revd Rosie Austin, the priest in the Shirwell Mission Community who, following a trip to Thika in Kenya (a Link Diocese for the Diocese of Exeter), began to implement what she saw there: Umoja, the word for 'together' in Swahili. The belief was that they had all they needed, and together church and community began to bring about positive change.

Rural communities feel the pressure of reduction in attendance, reduction in the number of clergy and aging buildings. In the midst of this Tom offers us the opportunity to think more deeply about the theology of the rural church and how the rhythms of its life and liturgy come to shape and be shaped by its communities.

This book, like the people in our rural churches, is a blessing to the Body of Christ for those of us in urban contexts as much as the rural church itself.

The Rt Revd Dame Sarah Mullally
Bishop of London

Preface

Circumstance rather than design has meant that almost all of this book has been written during the rather extraordinary Covid-19 pandemic of 2020–21. A glance at my notes reminds me that I began writing the manuscript on Trinity Sunday 2020, some ten weeks into the first lockdown. I am writing this Preface during Lent 2021, with the nation once again in lockdown, and very many churches closed. Doubtless in years to come this period in the history of the worshipping life of the Church will be studied and reflected on for all sorts of reasons. It is asking us a particular set of questions about the nature of our worshipping life. These questions, which are theological, doctrinal, ecclesiological, legal and sociological, apply to all worshipping communities. There is, however, something that speaks deeply into the heart of what this book is about: the nature and distinctiveness of rural worship.

Rural Christian communities, as this book will unpack, have a particular relationship with place. The church building is of course one 'place' that is profoundly significant. So too is the village or hamlet. For the multi-parochial benefice there is an important, and often complicated, relationship between the several residential communities that now share a priest, ministry team and service rota.

The restrictions upon common life and common worship over the past year mean that all the relationships I have just mentioned are in a high state of stress. The restrictions on access to buildings, and indeed the restrictions on mobility and the meeting of Christian people, made Lent, Holy Week and Eastertide 2020 like no other we have experienced in living memory. As I write, we are making plans for a second unusual

Holy Week. Our assumptions about what it means to be a worshipping community have been tried, tested and, in some places, found lacking. We are having to ask questions we have not asked for generations. We are rediscovering bits of doctrine we have not had recourse to for a century.

This is a book about worshipping as a rural community. More particularly it is a book about keeping the high days and holy days, the seasons and texture of the Christian year in rural Christian communities. It is significant that I am writing it at a point when Christian people have not met together to worship in their buildings with anything like the regularity and ease which had, until last year, simply been taken for granted. None of the great rites of Holy Week and Easter were celebrated in public in 2020. Today is the Feast of Saint Joseph, just a few weeks away from Easter 2021, and even in those churches that are gathering for public worship, masks, social distancing and a moratorium on congregational singing ensure that the experience is peculiar, unsettling and challenging.

I don't believe that anything I had planned to write in this book has been negated by the Covid-19 pandemic. Indeed, I think the need for this book has been proven. We have to dig deeper into what it means to be a rural Christian community, to grapple with and revel in that distinctiveness. We have to dig deeper into what it means to worship God too. This book is a meagre offering, but perhaps appears at an opportune moment. I pray that I never live through another such Holy Week. I pray, more importantly, that every Holy Week from now on is the better for the experience.

Tom Clammer OC
Salisbury, Feast of St Joseph, 2021

Introduction

This is a book about the way in which the rural church prays. It is a book about faith and about how Christians in the countryside celebrate and reflect upon that faith together.

It is a book that springs from personal experience of the Church of England in its distinctive configuration as rural worshipping communities. Growing up in a rural multi-parochial benefice in the south of the Diocese of Gloucester, my formative praying context was the village Church of England primary school, four small congregations in Victorian church buildings and a diet of worship drawn from the *Book of Common Prayer* (BCP) and the more contemporary liturgical expressions of the *Alternative Service Book* (ASB) and then latterly *Common Worship* (CW).

Leaving home for university, I spent the next ten years primarily worshipping in city centre or suburban parishes, first in Brighton where I read geography at university, then in south London where I spent a year working as a parish assistant, followed by three years in and around Cambridge during formation at Wescott House and then serving my title in a northern suburb of Gloucester. Throughout those ten years I returned regularly, and eagerly, to what I have always considered to be my home parish: that little cluster of rural churches in the parish of Tidenham with Beachley and Lancaut (see Fig. 1, p. xxv). I was fortunate enough to continue to sing in the parish choir occasionally during my university years and then latterly to be invited to conduct worship and to preach during my theological training. I don't think it is overstating it to say that *de facto* I have tended subconsciously to treat the Church of England in the rural context as the benchmark against which I gauge all the other encounters I have with the Anglican church in our country. To say that is not to devalue the other wonderful contexts in which Church of England Christians worship, or in which I have been privileged to exercise ministry, but simply to recognize that my formative experience has formed me, if you will pardon the tautology! We are shaped by our experience, some of which is geographical, and that is one recurring theme of this book.

Having served my curacy in the city of Gloucester, in October 2008 I was installed as priest-in-charge of the Severnside Benefice (see Fig. 2, p. xxix), a group of rural parishes held in plurality, with a remarkably diverse worshipping style, an interesting geography and a varied history.

Now, in an unexpected and rather unwelcome retirement from full-time stipendiary ministry for reasons of ill-health, I am once again privileged to find myself exercising my priesthood in a rural community. In a curious piece of ecclesiological symmetry, I am now an honorary associate priest in the parish of Tidenham! That context has of course changed over the years since I first began to exercise some leadership of worship as a teenager tentatively exploring the possibility of a vocation to the priesthood and there is much to reflect on in the development.

I offer this book as a contribution to the conversation about rural worship and rural ministry. It is not, primarily, a geographical or sociological analysis of rural communities, although there is something of that in what will follow. Neither is this book primarily an academic study of ecclesiology or liturgy, although having a robust appreciation of the liturgical life of the Church and a realistic and imaginative ecclesiology of rural communities is essential for a rural church that wants to pray well. Third, this book is not principally a set of resources for rural worship. As we go along I will offer ideas, and where appropriate I will point to the most recent resources which are aimed specifically at rural congregations. The problem with too much of that approach is of course that resources go out of date and excellent new material is being produced all the time. For that reason, my specific recommendations will be limited.

This is a book about how the rural church prays. It is primarily a liturgical theology of the rural Church of England, rooted in a deep belief that in order to pray well, the Church of England needs to know and understand its liturgy and know and understand its context. That is the recipe for any church beginning to pray effectively. That recipe is not limited to the rural church of course, and indeed the model I propose here could be adapted and used to analyse and examine suburban or urban contexts just as easily. It is, however, the rural church that, I find as I settle into retirement, has always had the first call upon my heart, because it is the context that formed me, the context that nurtured my vocation and the context to which I have returned.

The structure of this book is simple, but deliberate. The reader ought, of course, to feel free to dip in and out of what I offer, but it might be helpful for you to understand the direction of my thinking. My argument hangs around three assertions:

1 We could do better at thinking about a theology of the rural church.
2 We could do better at thinking about the way the rhythms and shape of the Christian year can build Christian community.
3 We could do *much* better at thinking about the way (1) and (2) relate.

We begin with context. Context is always critical. It is not the only thing that is critical, or the only thing that is important, but where we are shapes us. Some of that is practical: rural communities are likely to have more buildings, numerically fewer people and particular challenges and blessings. I begin by offering a brief pen portrait of two rural contexts in which most of my ministry has been undertaken. The Parish of Tidenham is where I have ministered both as a layperson discovering the treasury of faith and now as a retired honorary associate priest. The second context is the Severnside Benefice, where I had the privilege of holding the cure of souls. Both of these contexts are of course subjective, but both have good things to teach us about how we pray. I hope these portraits and examples will add a little colour to our conversation and help you to orient yourself in the moments where I offer some practical examples. Following those sketches, Chapter 1 addresses the question of context and argues for a carefully thought through ecclesiology of the rural church.

The next thing is our liturgical theology and this is the focus of Chapter 2. If context is vital for understanding the specific and distinctive aspects of our praying community, then our liturgical theology provides us with, in a sense, what is unchanging, or permanent. This is going to be a book that will appeal most to those who see an intrinsic value in 'the Tradition'. This book unashamedly claims that the liturgical inheritance of the Church of England, the deposit of faith contained within the BCP, and, in our own time, *Common Worship*, together with the surrounding rubrics, notes and commentary, and that more difficult to pin down and slightly nebulous 'Anglican way of doing things', provide something more than a static set of rules and formularies. They are the gift to the present from the past. They are the inheritance of faith which provide us with the principal source of our doctrine, as well as a set of expectations, understandings and shared promises about how we will *be* when we worship together. The Church of England is most itself when it is joined together in common prayer.

Bringing the context together with our liturgical theology creates what is usually known as *praxis*. In other words, it creates that interaction between God and the people which is lived theology, expressed in worship, prayer, praise, teaching, learning, grieving, growing and loving God and each other as community. Chapters 3, 4 and 5 are an outworking of the first two chapters. Having thought about our community, and having thought about our liturgy, we will bring them together. I examine the Christmas cycle first, followed by the Easter cycle, and then conclude with some exploration of the distinctly rural, or agricultural, festivals. That said, most of what will be said is transferable and ideas that are offered in one chapter may very well be applicable to other times, places or seasons. One of the characteristics of many rural parishes is a significant increase in attendance at these festival periods, which can be juxtaposed with a relatively low attendance at other times of the year, made the more prominent by the small population size of many of our communities. In this itself we are reminded of that call from Scripture and the ordination service to 'preach the word in season and out of season' (2 Tim. 4.2; *Common Worship: Ordination Services* (CW: OS), p. 37), which might have a particularly tangible realism about it in the rural context.

I should say a word about terminology. I am likely to use the titles parish, benefice, group, team and multi-parochial benefice fairly interchangeably. I am aware of the differences, both legal and structural, between them all, and wherever that is important I will lay that out explicitly. On other occasions, any and all of these terms can be read as generally referring to a community of Christians in a broadly rural context, gathering together for prayer and worship, probably in more than one church building.

All scriptural quotations and references are from the *New Revised Standard Version* of the Bible unless otherwise stated.

Finally, a word on the title of this book. *Crowning the Year* is inspired by the Collect for Harvest Thanksgiving in *Common Worship* (p. 521). The phrase is lifted from Psalm 65.11. Bradshaw traces the prayer to the 1989 South African Prayer Book (p. 222). In this prayer we are reminded that it is God who crowns our endeavours. Our ministry, though blessed and hallowed by God, is always a response to the gift freely given: that we are invited into the great congregation of angels and saints that surround the throne of God and are privileged to join our voices with that unending hymn of praise. That is the calling of every Christian and the promise held out to every person. As Christians who do some, most, or all of our praying in the countryside, our duty and joy is to work together to tune our collective antennae to that song of the angels, to notice from which direction the heavenly chorus is drifting towards us and to do our best to join our song with theirs as God, in his mercy and his grace, crowns our years with his goodness.

Eternal God,
you crown the year with your goodness
and you give us the fruits of the earth in their season:
grant that we may use them to your glory,
for the relief of those in need and for our own well-being;
through Jesus Christ your Son our Lord,
who is alive and reigns with you,
in the unity of the Holy Spirit,
one God, now and for ever. Amen.

Pen Portraits of Two Rural Communities

Picture, if you will, a couple of rural Christian communities. From time to time I will draw on these two parishes in order to provide some concrete illustrations from my own ministry. What follows is not a full historical or demographic analysis of these places, but just a thumbnail sketch. I am also focusing almost entirely upon the provision of public worship in church buildings or other public places, in the geographical environment. It is important to note that I am not providing a complete summary of the life, nature or ministry of the parishes. Please read with the caveats always in your mind that I am not the incumbent of either of these communities (though once upon a time I was priest-in-charge of the Severnside Benefice and I am currently an honorary associate priest in Tidenham) and that the examples and background that I share are inevitably coloured by my own memory and experience. My apologies to the current incumbents, and the people, for any inaccuracy of recollection. Both these communities are places where I have had the privilege to serve as a priest and both of them have formed me very deeply in different ways.

Tidenham Parish

I will use 'Tidenham Parish' as shorthand at various points. The full title is 'the Parish of Tidenham with Beachley and Lancaut' and it is held in plurality by the current incumbent with the Parish of St Briavels with Hewelsfield and Brockweir.

In adopting shorthand for ease of repetition, I am acutely aware that by doing so, and choosing to use one title as a catch-all, I collude in one of those dangerous behaviours in rural ministry, which is to nest a whole bunch of diverse and distinctive communities under the title of one village. Let the reader be assured that I am aware of this, and feel appropriately uncomfortable!

Located in the Diocese of Gloucester, in the Archdeaconry of Gloucester and the Deanery of Forest South, this community constitutes two separate legal parishes, currently held in plurality by one stipendiary incumbent who lives in Tutshill (see Figure 1, p. xxv). The patron of the Parish of Tidenham is the bishop. The patron of the Parish of St Briavels with Hewelsfield and Brockweir is the Dean and Chapter of Hereford.

I grew up in these communities, attended the primary school in Tutshill and then secondary school in Sedbury. Throughout my university years and subsequent training for ordination, I returned regularly to the parishes and began to exercise some ministry as an ordinand, then later as an occasional visiting priest. It was worshipping in these rural churches that fostered my Christian faith, and subsequently my vocation to ordination, and I feel strongly to this day that these villages and these churches are my spiritual home. It is a delight, in retirement, to be able to minister slightly more regularly among the people of Tidenham.

When I first knew the parishes, they were not held in plurality. The Parish of Tidenham with Beachley and Lancaut had a full-time stipendiary priest. In 1995 there were four open buildings: the parish church of St Mary and St Peter, Tidenham, and chapels of ease at Tutshill, Tidenham Chase and Beachley. St John the Evangelist, Beachley, closed in the summer of 1998. There are two further ruined chapels within the parish boundary: the rather extraordinary chapel of St Tecla, stranded on an island at the end of Beachley Point, and the ruined church of St James the Great, Lancaut, down on the banks of the River Wye, which is used about once a year for open-air worship.

The main population centre in modern times is Tutshill, which sits at the junction of the two primary roads within the

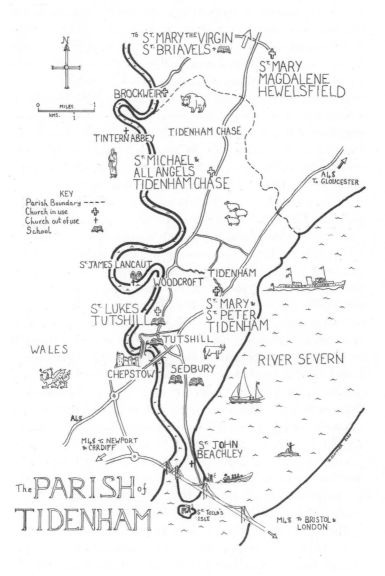

Figure 1: Map of Tidenham Parish

parish, the A48 running up the River Severn to Gloucester, and the B4228 running north along the River Wye. The parishes form a wedge, largely contained by these two roads. The roads follow the course of two principal rivers: the River Wye and the River Severn, which themselves lend a distinctive identity to this area. They form the southernmost part of the Diocese of Gloucester on the north bank of the River Severn and as such they look at least as much into Wales, particularly towards the town of Chepstow, as they do towards Gloucester. The only railway line in the parish runs north-east along the bank of the River Severn towards Gloucester and connects the area with that city and Birmingham, as well as the principal settlements of South Wales such as Newport, Cardiff and Swansea.

There are a significant number of retired residents and those who work are largely commuters. There is some agriculture practised and there are some significant portions of Forestry Commission land, parts of the historic Royal Forest of Dean, contained within the parish boundary as well. This brings a degree of tourism and leisure into the parishes. The parish contains five schools, Church of England primaries in Tutshill and St Briavels, a primary school in Sedbury, an independent prep school in Tutshill, Wyedean secondary school in Sedbury and two large toddler groups. Of these schools, the one in St Briavels retains a distinctly rural feel, while the others have more the feel of town schools and draw from a catchment which includes pupils from across the national border in Wales. Regular acts of worship have been provided in all schools by members of the ministry team and other lay Christians. Two fresh expressions of church have been operating in recent years: one in St Briavels and one in Sedbury.

The Parish of St Briavels with Hewelsfield and Brockweir was added to the cure of the vicar of Tidenham in 2005, but the parishes have not been united. The two parishes are held in plurality by the incumbent, who is priest-in-charge of the more recent additions, and vicar of Tidenham. In recent years there have been moves towards fostering something of a 'united benefice' identity, including sharing the ministry of clergy and lay people, particularly during the 2020 coronavirus pandemic, providing online worship and online opportunities for prayer that have been taken up by people from across the parishes.

There are resident self-supporting curates in St Briavels and Tidenham, a resident reader in Hewelsfield, a resident stipendiary curate in Tutshill, with two further readers living in the parish of Tidenham.

Every church within the parishes usually hosts an act of worship on a Sunday. Provision varies from an entirely BCP diet at Tidenham Chase, through a mixed economy of Prayer Book and *Common Worship* at Tidenham and St Briavels, to an entirely contemporary language set of services at Tutshill and Hewelsfield. Holy Communion is celebrated in each church at least once a month and weekly in Tidenham and St Briavels. Church tradition varies from full Eucharistic vestments in some churches to expectation that no distinctive vesture will be worn for worship in other buildings except for the Eucharist. There is very little Sunday evening worship offered, with only one church, Tidenham Chase, regularly hosting an evening service. Midweek Eucharistic worship in church has historically been infrequent, though currently a regular midweek Eucharist is being trialled in Tutshill. The morning Office is recited Monday to Thursday, with three of those services migrating around the churches, and an online opportunity, at the time of writing, on a Tuesday. An arrangement of home groups meeting for study, worship and fellowship operates in and around Tutshill.

Average Sunday attendance varies from a dozen or so in the smaller villages to somewhere in the region of 75 in Tutshill.

The Severnside Benefice

Situated in the north of the Diocese of Gloucester, in the Deanery of Tewkesbury and Winchcombe, the Severnside Benefice comprises four parishes held in plurality by one part-time incumbent. The parishes are those of Deerhurst with Apperley; Chaceley; Forthampton, and Tredington with Stoke Orchard, each with its own PCC (see Fig. 2, p. xxix). These parishes lie between Gloucester and Tewkesbury, in what is known as the Severn Vale. The parishes are almost entirely rural, with farming still a significant local occupation. Some of the farms are privately owned, and some are tenancies. Patronage of the parishes is split between the bishop (Deerhurst, and Tredington), a private patron (Forthampton) and the Vicar of Longden (Chaceley).

The most profound and significant geographical feature of the parishes is that the collective benefice is divided into three by one natural and one man-made feature. If you glance at Figure 2 you will see that the parishes of Forthampton and Chaceley are divided from the rest of the benefice by the River Severn, which runs pretty much north-south on its way down to the sea at Bristol. Although there are bridges by which the river can be crossed, neither of the two nearest bridges lie within the parishes themselves, so it is impossible to travel from the westernmost part of the benefice to the central or easternmost part without leaving the ecclesiastical parish. The river provides the benefice with its informal 'Severnside' title, and certainly while I was incumbent there was a strapline which appeared on much of the publicity: 'by the Severn divided, by the Spirit united', which attempted to acknowledge and theologize upon this significant geographical impediment. The Parish of Deerhurst has been held in plurality with the parishes of Forthampton and Chaceley for some significant period of time and although there is folk memory of the time when parishes had something more closely approximating 'our own vicar', that has not been the case for many decades.

There is a second significant geographical feature, this time wrought by human hands. The M5 motorway runs north-south, mirroring the course of the River Severn, and divides the central part of the benefice from the Parish of Tredington with Stoke Orchard. Although there is a motorway bridge within the parish, nonetheless the motorway is a significant psychological presence and while the parishes in the western and central part of the benefice tend to look north to Tewkesbury as their most local population centre, on the other side of the M5 there is naturally a pull towards the local town of Bishop Cleeve and thence Cheltenham. The easternmost parish was added to the

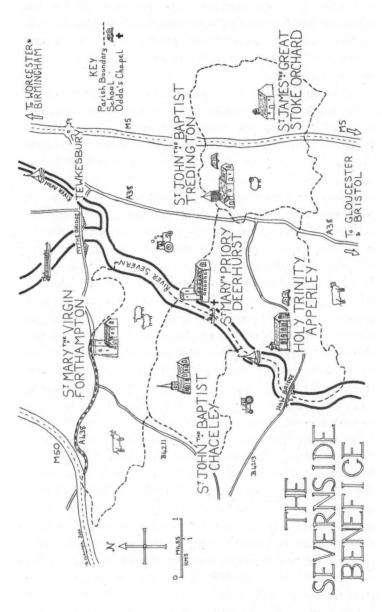

Figure 2: Map of the Severnside Benefice

cure of the Vicar of Deerhurst in 1998, having previously found its pastoral provision elsewhere. The presence of the M5 and the River Severn mean that more significant work needs to be put into fostering a sense of benefice identity than might have appeared when the parishes were united in a desktop exercise in a diocesan office.

Agriculture remains a significant employer in the area, with active farms in all the parishes, and farmers featuring among the regular worshippers. There is also some commuting north to Tewkesbury, south to Gloucester, as well as further afield. The relative ease of travel via the M5 motorway allows commuting out of the diocese and county. Certainly during my time there was a growing prevalence of homeworking. There is a significant retired population. In addition, a settled traveller community in Tredington provided a particular and distinctive residential community. Two primary schools, one in Apperley (Church of England) and one in Tredington (Community) provided education for the majority of the younger children. There is no secondary school within the benefice, with older children tending to travel to Tewkesbury, Cheltenham or Gloucester for their secondary education. A significant difference with Tidenham Parish, whose settlements tend to cluster on the main roads, is that for the villages of Chaceley, Forthampton and Deerhurst, there is virtually no through traffic. These villages sit away from the main roads, which necessarily alters the social geography. Even Apperley, the largest village by population, sits away from the B4213. None of the villages lie on the A38, which is the main road from Gloucester to Tewkesbury. The only significant through traffic passes along the minor road which runs from the A38 to Bishops Cleeve through Tredington and Stoke Orchard. The part-time priest-in-charge resides in Apperley, where a self-supporting minister also lives. There is a reader living in Forthampton, and another reader living in Tredington. Members from across the benefice are part of a Local Ministry Team who undertake various pastoral and liturgical ministries.

The liturgical life of the benefice was certainly broad during my incumbency. Of the six church buildings, three had altars in the traditional position against the east wall of the sanctuary and the Eucharist was celebrated facing east. I maintained that practice in all three of those churches, while in one church moving the altar westward slightly to facilitate Eucharist facing the people on occasions such as baptisms. Two churches had altars which had already been relocated to allow west-facing celebration. The significant Saxon Deerhurst church, the most ancient of the churches in the benefice, boasts an extraordinary example of a post-Reformation chancel, with the altar table freestanding in the middle of the chancel and pew benches surrounding it on three sides. The furniture is Victorian, but when the furniture was replaced the Reformation arrangement was retained. This allowed the Eucharist to be celebrated to the letter of the BCP rubrics, with the altar aligned east-west, and the president standing at the long north side of the table, facing south. This arrangement was not popular with the regular congregation and so I used to celebrate occasionally, but rarely, in that arrangement. Most of the time the altar was oriented in the more familiar north-south position, but still freestanding with the congregation arranged around it. On most Sundays during my incumbency I would celebrate at least one BCP service and one CW service; there would also be non-Eucharistic Services of the Word, some of which would be celebrated without any distinctive vesture. There was a small benefice choir which provided simple choral accompaniment and hymns were common fare. The congregation at Tredington was the most keen on exploring the more modern repertoire of worship songs and worship was regularly accompanied by guitar in that church.

The regular monthly service rota provided that there would be at least one Eucharist within the benefice each Sunday and on most Sundays there would be at least two Communion services. Two Sundays a month there was the opportunity to worship in the evening, at BCP Evensong. Non-Eucharistic worship was available on at least two Sundays a month and these services were usually lay led by a member of the Local Ministry Team which included two readers. In Apperley there was a happy and reasonably long-standing arrangement with the local Methodist chapel, whereby worship would alternate week by week between the chapel of ease in Apperley and the Methodist Chapel. There was some ecumenical working together during Lent and on occasions such as Remembrance Sunday. This was somewhat developed during my incumbency to embrace more creative shared liturgies, particularly the Palm Sunday procession.

I inherited no tradition of regular midweek worship. For the period of my incumbency I introduced the Daily Offices, and for a period of a couple of years also attempted, unsuccessfully, to introduce a midweek Eucharist. There was a tradition of forming a group for prayer and study during Lent, which was ecumenical.

Average Sunday attendances varied from four or five at some BCP services to perhaps 20 or so at CW Eucharist services. On 'fifth Sundays', where the tradition was to hold a benefice service which would rotate around the six churches, the attendance would perhaps be 30 or so, which constituted the largest single congregation of the quarter, but a significant reduction on the average Sunday attendance across the benefice.

Being Rural: An Ecclesiology of the Rural Benefice

Starting with the Incarnation

Just as the liturgical year is given its shape by the celebrations of Easter and Christmas, so this book will reflect the constant dialogue between the Incarnation and the Resurrection that forms our understanding of the nature and person of Christ and therefore heavily influences his Church. It is possible to see parallels between Chapters 1 and 2, which discuss ecclesiology and liturgical theology respectively, and our discussion of Christmas and Easter in Chapters 3 and 4. There is something distinctly incarnational about considering the located church, just as there is something about the primacy and defining nature of the Resurrection which is shot through all our public worship. To push this relationship too far would be a mistake, since of course, just as one cannot divide Christ's humanity and divinity, to try to hold too much clear water between the Incarnation and the Resurrection would be to tiptoe on the very edge of heresy. Nonetheless, it is true that our first exploration here into what it means to be a rural Christian community is going to draw on a good deal of our theology of place and identity, which has something of the Incarnation about it. Just so, when we begin to think about what the church prays publicly, we will become very conscious of the resurrection trumpets.

'The Bible makes it abundantly clear that God starts where people are' (Jones and Martin, p. 17). All ministry is done in context. This might seem to be a statement of the staggeringly obvious, but it is one of the two assertions at the heart of this book. Whenever God interacts with creation, there is a union, a mingling, of the eternal and the transient. The great mystery of the Incarnation, which we retell every Christmas, is the ultimate and perfect expression of this union between God and creation: 'And the Word became flesh and dwelt among us' (John 1.14). In Christ we see what perfect union with God looks like. Our ministry of course, although done for love of God, in the name of Christ, and in the power of the Holy Spirit, has to try rather harder to make sense of the mystery of the union between us and God.

We do our praying where we are. For mortal, corporeal humanity that necessarily means our praying is geographical. We must be sitting, standing or kneeling somewhere to pray. Whether in a home, a church building, on the train, on a park bench or in a thousand other contexts, our prayer is located; it is geographical. Not only that, but even in a highly digitized world, a lot of our living is still geographical. Despite the extraordinary revolution in communications in recent decades, exponentially increased by the 2020 coronavirus pandemic, we are still physically somewhere when we connect, by whatever electronic means, with our friends, families and workplaces. Communities exist. Many of those communities became much smaller in March 2020 as the entire nation was locked down. Some communities discovered imaginative ways of reconstituting themselves partially on the World Wide Web or through conferencing software. Some communities struggled desperately with this sort of technology and have felt on the brink of collapse. All communities, I would suggest, felt the pain of the lockdown and that is because the geographical element is still highly significant.

I am not the only priest who has commented on the significant pastoral pain of not being able to shake hands with the congregation at the church door (at the time of writing this is still prohibited under social distancing guidelines). There is something physical, something tangible and grounding, as well as something which is simply deeply instinctive, about human touch. That is connected to the other things about geography: we belong in a place, with a people, and that place and those people matter. They are part of who we are and we are part of who they are.

The purpose of this chapter is to acknowledge the truth of our 'locatedness' and to ask how a distinctively rural identity might shape our ecclesiology. In other words, what is it about being a rural Christian community, perhaps a small parish or, more likely, group of parishes, which makes how we 'do' our Christianity distinct? When we think about ecclesiology we are thinking about the nature of the church. Some of the things we probably want to say about the church are universal, or perhaps are universal but interpreted and mediated nationally in the case of the Church of England. One of those things is our liturgy and Chapter 2 is all about how we marry authorized national liturgy with context. Other things are much more local. There are things about identity as a diocese, or perhaps as a geographical region such as a county. Some parts of our identity are significantly more local than that and have to do with history, physical geography, patterns of employment, commuting, education and migration.

One of the things it is vital to remember is that God revels in that identity. We know God rejoices and delights in the created order (Prov. 8.31), and what is central to that creation is humanity. It is not a historical accident that the Word became flesh in a particular place at a particular time. There is something about the Incarnation that is all about the experience of an eternal, transcendent, omnipotent, omnipresent God in a particular place, at a particular time, which shows us how it is that God comes close to us.

Building our ecclesiology

As we begin to develop an ecclesiology of the rural church, we need to say some things about God and some things about being rural. There are a number of excellent studies which have done a good deal of this work and I will point to them in the course of what follows. It is a very good thing that there are a number of ways into this question of what rural Christianity might be like, because that means the individual minister, pastoral team or PCC is likely to be able to find a methodology which appeals to them and will help to unpack the issues for discussion. That is really the aim of this book: that the questions I pose here, and the beginnings of the answers that this study moves towards, might inspire people in their own context to have these conversations around the PCC table, or perhaps in small groups, and see where the conversation takes them.

We have to begin with some principles, and those that underpin this chapter are these:

1 God is entirely and eternally love, and that does not change.
2 We, as human beings, experience God's eternal love contextually.

Because we hold both to be true, it explains and gives us a mandate to expect that the way in which a community encounters God in a particular context will be, to some extent, specific. This is not because God changes, but rather because humanity is contextual.

We therefore expect that the Church, which is the manifestation of the body of Christ on earth, will also be contextual and might look, feel and do things differently depending on its context. There are a set of eternal and everlasting truths revealed by God through the Church, but those eternal and everlasting truths are transmitted, received and proclaimed by a church that is local as well as universal.

So, what might the principles be in relation to the rural church? I would like to suggest that the following might be a useful starting point:

1 Physical geography matters.
2 Social geography matters.
3 A small church is not the same as a failed large church.
4 There are things to learn from the model of cell church.
5 There are things to learn from the monastic (or Religious) tradition.
6 We need to be confident about our strengths.
7 We need to be honest about our weaknesses.

These seven principles will guide the rest of this chapter. Before that, however, there is one other 'big picture' aspect which is worth acknowledging.

I wouldn't start from here!

I remember a visioning exercise that was undertaken in one of the rural contexts in which I have ministered. We began the day by spreading out a large map of the benefice on a table and identifying the various church buildings, the schools, the areas of most substantial population, the main geographical features, the access routes for transport, and so on. One of the repeated comments from those of us in that group was, 'Well, if I was beginning a Christian community on this patch of the vineyard, I wouldn't start from *here!*' I think it is worth acknowledging that from the outset, because it is a feeling that is encountered by many in rural ministry. Faced with the challenge of a piece of geography within the Church of England, and unlimited money and resources, there would be a strong argument for arranging the buildings, and other facilities, in a very different configuration from that which we have inherited. At least one of us around the table suggested that one large church at the geographical centre point of the area, with a large car park, would be a far more sensible way of organizing Christian ministry in this particular area and there is a good deal of truth in that.

We start, however, from where we are, which is largely with a set of churches built in a period where transport was significantly less easy, affordable and ubiquitous than it is now, when population centres were smaller and there was less regular migration between them, and when the funding of church buildings came from a variety of sources, not least from private landowners.

If we are people of the Incarnation then we know God meets us where we are, and what we have inherited is just as much God's gift as that which we might develop or create in our own time. It is in that spirit the rest of this chapter unfolds.

1 Physical geography matters

The General Synod report *Seeds in Holy Ground*, published in 2005, began by confidently drawing the attention of the local church to its context. The first question posed in that rather fine workbook was, 'Where are we now?' (GS Misc 803, p. 4). Although the data cited in *Seeds* are now well out of date, the methodology is sound and repays another reading. PCCs and teams who looked at this report at the time may well find that pulling it out and dusting it off again would be a good starting point. Apart from anything else, the title of the report itself is deeply theological and sets the scene well for all the work that has followed since then.

Seeds refers to 'the importance of place' (p. 11), and much of the later writing picks up on this theme. Sally Gaze, writing shortly after *Seeds*, identifies the deep rhythms and nature of the rural community which lend parish churches in the country-side something of a distinctive identity. She notes that they are:

> Naturally drawn to an incarnational approach in that they are inheritors of a tradition that has sought to build on people's innate spirituality rather than dismiss it as inadequate or superstitious. For example, the celebration of harvest and rogation can be seen as the churches' attempts to respond incarnationally to the deep awareness of the natural world. (Gaze, p. 10)

Again, the word 'incarnational' is used to try to express something of the way in which God and context meet together to form a distinctive experience of the expression of faith.

Honey and Thistles is not primarily an ecclesiological study of rural Christianity, but rather a creative and refreshing approach to looking at farming through the lens of Scripture. It is well worth reading by anyone interested in a rigorously biblical approach to agriculture in the modern age. It does contain within it, however, a couple of real nuggets of ecclesiology. The authors, Jones and Martin, are clear, as am I, that the nature of God doesn't change from place to place. Nonetheless, a particular context can heighten, or make particularly clear, a universal truth. One of the particular ministries of the rural church is to witness to the whole Church, and to the world, the centrality of the natural world to God's redeeming purposes:

> There are some Christians who see concern with the natural world as a distraction from 'spiritual matters'. It seems to us that the Bible does not support such a view. There are profound reasons why there are flowers in church and for the celebration of land related festivals such as rogation and harvest. The care of churchyards can also reflect this pattern of relationships. There is potential for thankfulness and joy in these relationships but also, of course, for pain and loss. The natural world does not always cherish us. The Bible does not offer easy explanations for this, but it is completely realistic about the existence of the tough bits. It sees all the relationships as interconnected and mutually sustaining or distorting each other. (Jones and Martin, pp. 110–11)

So, there are some dominant ecclesiological themes in rural communities that flow from the physical environment in which Christian praying happens. They are not exclusive to rural communities and rural communities are not *better* or *worse* than suburban or urban contexts because of them. Nonetheless, these ecclesiological themes are present and we do well to recognize and embrace them, because they will help to form us in our praying and in all the witnessing, mission and pastoral care which will flow from that praying. These dominant ecclesiological themes have to do with the natural world, with rhythms and cycles, with creation and with community.

We ought not to move on from considering the physical environment without acknowledging that this includes the fabric of our church buildings. I have sat in too many meetings of the Diocesan Advisory Committee to ever forget the oft repeated mantra: 'the building will always win.' Later on, in the chapters looking at the liturgies specifically, we will think more about the use of rural church buildings, but it pays to state at the outset that one of the distinctive things about much of rural ministry in the Church of England is the inheritance of a number of church buildings. As we noted earlier, in the Parish of Tidenham there were four buildings, one of which was closed during the period I worshipped there, and now two more buildings have been added to the cure of souls. In the Severnside Benefice where I was incumbent, we had six buildings, all of which were listed and one of which was Grade I. Going back to that conversation around a map of any set of rural communities, we may not instinctively have started by building four, six, or in some cases dozens of expensive, high-maintenance and often quite large church buildings all over our patch. We may well have opted to build one big, well-insulated and low-maintenance building in the geographical centre, with some really excellent toilet facilities, breakout rooms, catering facilities and a car park. I don't think anyone would begrudge the rural incumbent or churchwarden that daydream while reclining in a deck chair on holiday somewhere! We are, however, where we are. What we have received are buildings which, as many have commented in previous writings, are often highly visible, prominent and can serve as icons or reminders of holiness. Sometimes, of course, they are in the wrong place, or ugly, or in such a state of dilapidation that they cannot be used. Either way, we have a significant number of buildings to factor into our ecclesiology of rural ministry and that needs to be done carefully, and prophetically. Again, that strong incarnational strand runs through the theology of the rural church. A cluster of dwellings, perhaps a school, gathered around the spire or tower of the country church is an icon of the presence of God in the midst of the people. There is something here of the various characters in the nativity story gathered around the manger. All the outbuildings, animals and fields gathered around the farmhouse. As Jones and Martin put it, 'the pattern of family and farm under God mirrors this overall pattern of humans, creation and God all in a relationship with each other. It can be a sort of paradigm of the big picture' (Jones and Martin, p. 111).

2 Social geography matters

If it is vital to take account of the physical terrain when build-ing an ecclesiology of the rural church, it is equally vital to consider the people. I use the term 'social geography' to include all the questions around who physically lives in the parish, and where, together with questions of migration or commuting in and out of the parish, the demography of the people, the presence of one or more schools, of local businesses and of agri-culture. Vital, also, is where the parishes are located in relation to larger towns and cities, transport links and so on, together with all the spoken and unspoken loyalties and connections that might exist between individuals or groups. These can have a dramatic effect on the practical ecclesiology in a place. To cite just one example at this point: two principal roads bisect the Parish of Tidenham (see Fig. 1, p. xxix), carrying com-muters north to Gloucester, south into South Wales and up the border with Wales towards Monmouth. Conversely, in the Severnside Benefice, the vast majority of the settlements do not lie on the principal travel routes and several of the villages experience almost no through travel. This affects the nature of things like the presence of pubs and it has a significant effect on the potential visibility or otherwise of the churches and any advertising or promotional material that might be posted on church noticeboards, for example.

How we do our 'front-end' promotion of who we are and what we are doing is going to be influenced dramatically by whether or not anyone is likely to trip over the community or its church by accident or not. Also included under this bracket of social geography is the history of the community, which might include things that would fall under the umbrella of 'internal history': what has happened in the village, past joys and tragedies, past enmities or alliances. It will also encompass the history of the village in relation to its surrounding com-munities. If a particular parish within a united benefice has been passed from parish to parish seeking a permanent home, that has a profound effect upon the way in which that Christian community understands itself to be loved. If two parishes or churches with historically very different churchmanship or worshipping styles become part of a united benefice, that affects the ecclesiology as well.

Each person reading this section will recognize some of what I have just outlined, and perhaps also note where some of what I have said does not apply in their context. That is precisely the point: each community needs to understand its own ecclesiology, and each ecclesiology is affected or influenced by some or all of the above. There are some broader generalizations which can probably be made and these are summed up well by Jill Hopkinson, who notes that these distinctive aspects of rural ecclesiology have direct application to how ministry might happen:

> Rural churches and rural communities are different from those elsewhere. Small populations, the absence of public services, and travel distances and times all make a difference. Although many concepts and resources do not translate for use in rural church, some do ... There are also opportunities for mission and ministry that are not found in towns and cities. (Hopkinson in Martin, p. 13)

3 A small church is not the same as a failed big church

This is an absolutely vital piece of rural ecclesiology. It has almost become a mantra now, but I believe the first place it was written down was in *Seeds*, which noted that 'a small congregation is not a failed large one' (p. 26). Much angst is experienced by rural ministers or congregations falling into the trap of believing that the models operated by large suburban and city churches are equally applicable to the rural community. It is also true that from time to time, manuals, strategies and liturgical textbooks fail to take care to translate principles of mission, ministry or liturgy adequately to the rural multi-parochial context. Some of these models might include expectations about music, worship style, numbers in the congregation, design and use of worship space, outreach programmes, social media presence and much besides. I am not arguing that a rural community should ignore these considerations. They are all, in their way, integral to the ministry of any Christian community, but there has to be nuance and there must be an ecclesiology brought to bear first, rather than starting with a list of expected outputs which are actually derived from a very different ecclesiology. Rowan Williams, Archbishop of Canterbury at the time when he wrote this, noted:

> It will not do in our mission to assume that evangelism in the routine of worship in the countryside can or should be a straight transfer from urban, let alone suburban, patterns; some of the malaise and frustration that are felt in rural churches have to do with this, as well as with expectations that are brought in from elsewhere. (Williams in Gaze, p. x)

Rural Christian communities can be confident about their own identity, about their own ecclesiology, and this will mean that much of the modelling of mission and ministry will need to be translated, modified or reinterpreted for the rural parish. There will also be specific ecclesiological characteristics which the rural church excels in and which can be translated for suburban and urban communities.

What might some of these specific characteristics be? The following sections of this chapter will unwrap some of these which have to do with the nature of smaller, more local congregations, which do their praying in a distinctive manner formed by some of the physical and sociological factors that we have recently discussed. *Seeds* references Bishop Langrish as he describes some of the defining characteristics of a rural church as, 'incarnational, unifying, open doors, celebratory, light on structures, buildings taken seriously, but not a means to an end, a culture of nurture and growth, a spiritually growing people' (p. 4). In the same section the report notes the distinctive 'social capital' which may well be owned by rural churches due to the interrelationship with other organizations. The nature of village life is often that there is significantly greater overlap between organizations and groups within the community. Rural ministers will recognize my experience of villages in which the makeup of the PCC, village hall committee, Parish Council, school governing body and local cricket club overlapped significantly. In any community where there is less migration into any particular club or society, the boundaries between disparate communities become more porous. This presents its own set of challenges, but there is also a tremendous social capital to be treasured where the rural minister will see the same people in multiple settings and will be seen themselves in those settings. The investment in the presence of the parish church may well be very high, with all the goodwill and moral support that is carried with it, even if attendance at church on Sunday is numerically low. Residents of a rural community may very well not consider that attending church makes any difference to that church belonging to them. This was certainly an attitude which challenged me when I became a rural incumbent, but over time I began to understand that it makes sense when belonging is not understood so much as a positive active decision, but rather part of an assumed identity possessed by virtue of existing in that community.

The literature on the relationship between a rural church and its community is uneven. Nothing of what I have said above will be a particularly original addition to the discussion, but it is worth noting that an uncertainty and discomfort still exists among many about the legitimacy of very small rural congregations as active and engaged parts of the Christian community. Part of this has to do with problems in translation. Language of mission and evangelism carries with it a certain set of assumptions which can switch a rural congregation off, perhaps unjustly. Similarly, some of the more recent literature seeks to acknowledge the distinctive nature of rural communities, but then slips back, almost subconsciously, into suburban evangelical models. One interesting example worth considering is that presented by Hobbs, himself both a geographer and a house-for-duty priest. He presents a really interesting and challenging account of his own experience among rural communities in the Diocese of Guildford and offers a particularly thought-provoking definition of his context in terms of the three identities: geographical, historical and spiritual (Hobbs, pp. 4–5). This might well offer a useful model for other communities seeking to build an ecclesiology. As his account develops, however, a number of distinctly suburban evangelical models present themselves, for example in the use of term cards, systematic Bible preaching, flagship services, the use of the Alpha course, moving away from traditional liturgical forms and so on (pp. 26–7). None of these, of course, are in themselves bad things to do, but it does read a little like importing the suburban model and trying to make it fit into a rural context.

What is not needed is for rural churches to stubbornly close their ears and eyes to what is happening more widely in the Church of England. To do that is to stay firmly in denial. It is, however, vital that as a rural church observes the life of the wider church, it is able to do so from a confident ecclesiological base, having a clear understanding of who and what they are, so that models, practices and systems can emerge which are contextual, honouring the physical geography of the place, aware and reactive to the social geography, and confident in the distinctive particular ministry of a small church, which is not a failed large church, but which expresses a particular and valuable ministry. The final four sections of this chapter offer some particular observations about what this emerging ecclesiology might value as part of that distinct identity.

4 There are things to learn from the model of cell church

Cell church, as an ecclesiological model within the Anglican churches of the British Isles, has been around for a good while now. It draws deeply from the biblical model of the church described by St Paul (1 Cor. 12; Col. 1.18 etc.), which presents the Church as the body of Christ, with Jesus as the head, and with the members of the church, with their distinctive ministries, as constituent parts of the body. Developing the Pauline teaching, cell church reminds us that a vital role of any living cell within the human body, or indeed other living things, is to grow, divide, and thus build up the body. A model of cell church is therefore interested in smaller units of Christian gathering as vital elements, because it is in these smaller group-ings, as in the cells of the human body, that the growth and division necessary for multiplication will happen. A typical cell model in a large suburban church would break the members of the Sunday congregations down into cells of perhaps a dozen, in which much of the fellowship, teaching and worship day by day would take place. Many of the cells will then come together once a week, typically on Sunday, to constitute the entire body, but the focus in terms of discipleship, prayer and learning is invested in the individual cells, who might meet in the homes of members of the congregation, in a local coffee shop, in a pub, or a dozen other locations.

Lack, writing about worship in rural settings, picks up on the model of cell church, and identifies three nesting sizes of gather-ing that might typically be identified in a large cell church: 'cell, congregation, celebration' (Lack, p. 4). He goes on to note, 'The weekly challenge in many rural churches is that they are in no man's land. They are meeting in little more than "cell" group numbers, but most people want "congregational" wor-ship'. This observation is perceptive and presents a challenge to rural ministry in terms of what expectations there are, par-ticularly around Sunday worship. What is the purpose of the Sunday act of worship in a village context? Is it to provide the 'shopfront' or 'shot in the arm' of religion that will sustain the members of the congregation through the week, or is what is going on more like what a midweek cell group meeting might be? Again, there is almost certainly no one simple answer to this question and context will have a huge part to play. I think that the observation about cell church is useful though, because it offers a rural ministry team a slightly different lens through which to view what might be taking place on a Sunday.

What might change if the entire united benefice is viewed as the congregation and each smaller worshipping community is viewed as a cell of that congregation? After all, in many rural parishes, including those in which I have ministered, sometimes Sunday congregations are only a dozen or fewer. This is approximately the size of the average cell group. Does the cell model still hold up, even if the entire congregation – the united benefice – almost never physically meet up? One of the perennial frustrations in many multi-parochial benefices is what happens on the fifth Sunday of the month, or equivalent, where quite often the regular Sunday schedule is suspended and a 'benefice' or 'team' service is offered instead, to which all the discrete congregations are invited. My own experience was that take up was always partial, and although four or five times a year I had a congregation that was perhaps 40 strong, rather than 15 or 20 strong, the total Sunday attendance on these occasions was lower than it would have been had I maintained the usual Sunday schedule. Perhaps the cell church model offers us a useful ecclesiological lens to explore this phenomenon. If at least part of the psychological identity of a member of the rural congregation is strongly focused on the building and the people of the particular village, this is an indication that part of what is going on when that person comes to church on a Sunday is a significant identification with that locality. This is comparable with the cell, in the cell church structure. The cell is where the vast majority of the discipleship, growth, challenge, prayer and nurture takes place because it is the natural unit of Christian identity. An awareness of the larger benefice, team or group is almost certainly there, and some of the benefits of that larger organizational structure are recognized, but it is not the natural place of encounter. I recognize some of this model, too, in conversations I have had with parishioners about the significance or importance of the deanery, archdeaconry, or diocese. We do well to recognize where there are instinctive bonds and ties of affection, identity and fellowship and seek to facilitate those being places where the reality of the incarnation can be nurtured.

A final comment on cell church before we move on to a related but distinctive lens: we do well to attend to the natural groupings in which people instinctively want to worship. Another temptation in rural ministry, certainly for me, has been to simplify and rationalize the acts of worship taking place on a Sunday. If one has four buildings in a benefice, why not have one service each Sunday, and rotate it around the benefice Sunday by Sunday? There are places where this is happening and works well. Where there is resistance, however, it might have to do with this instinctive identification with the local as the place where prayer happens most easily. Any of us who have worshipped for any period of time in a particular church building, or perhaps a favourite spot on the top of the hill or by the seaside, will recognize that there are places where we sink more easily and swiftly into prayer. Again, this is geographical, sociological and ecclesiological all at the same time. Because we are embodied people, and we pray in the physical world, it is natural there will be places where prayer comes more easily or naturally. For all that we want to encourage people to be able to pray in any circumstance, we know perfectly well we are just as embodied as anyone else. When I go to church I instinctively sit in pretty much the same place every time. That is not so much because I think of that place as 'my pew', but simply because if I am in that place, with a familiar view of the altar from a particular angle, surrounded by the stained glass I regularly look at for inspiration, I just find it easier to pray. In exactly the same way, I have a little prayer table to the left of my desk as I am typing this. On it is an icon and a candle and it is there that I say my daily Office. I could say my prayers anywhere in the house, but this is my sacred space. We need to take this seriously. While of course there is a place for challenge, sometimes robust challenge, to those who are disinclined ever to attend services outside their own village, locality does matter and the pain felt by being separated from that locality is at least partially real and at least partially a genuine ecclesiological pain. For this reason, the maintenance of some act of worship in most churches on most Sundays might well be quite important. Dow, in his study of leadership in rural churches, argues firmly for resistance to the temptation to reduce the number of acts of worship in a rural benefice. To reduce the number of services 'is to retreat in good order when what is needed is to advance in mission and growth. If this collusion is not broken, the rural churches will die' (Dow, p. 9). Maintaining a significant number of services each week does require energy, significant resource and potentially a reimagining of the type, scale and length of these acts of worship, as the likelihood of being able to sustain a sung parish Eucharist every Sunday in nine rural villages is low!

Taking cell church as part of an ecclesiological model moves us some way towards wrapping our heads around how rural worship might work. To complement and add to this model, we now turn our attention to what might, at first glance, appear to be an entirely different world: the monastic cloister.

5 There are things to learn from the monastic (or Religious) model

As we build our ecclesiology of the rural church, one of the things I want to attempt is to fuse the cell church model, with its emphasis on the small group as at the heart of Christian formation, with some insights from the monastic, or Religious, tradition. My, by now familiar, caveat about over-generalization needs to be restated here. I am acutely aware that every Religious community is subtly different from every other and that each particular tradition has subtly different emphases and associated practices. My own experience is broadly Benedictine. For almost 20 years I was a Companion of the Community of the Resurrection at Mirfield and found the charism of that community deeply enriching. I am now a novice in an Anglican Cistercian community, which expresses an essentially contemplative vocation, placing the threefold vows of obedience, stability and conversion of life within a distinctly reflective framework, at the heart of which is a commitment to staying still and sustaining the church and the world in contemplative prayer. My involvement in these Religious communities leads me to make a number of connections between the more 'cloistered' life of prayer and the more 'active' ministry of the parish. This in itself ought not to surprise us: liturgical study of the forms of prayer in the church as it emerged in the early centuries points us towards two broad traditions: that of the 'desert' and that of the 'city'. These two parallel traditions are sometimes also referred to as the 'monastic' and 'cathedral' traditions, pointing to the fact that both patterns of prayer seek to do broadly the same thing, but in a different context. Once again we find that context is crucial! The desert model of prayer is characterized by more, and longer, readings from Scripture, particularly from the psalter, with proportionally fewer liturgical ceremonies. It suited those who sought out the solitude of the desert in order to pursue a life of contemplation. My daily prayers now look more like this. In contrast, the cathedral or city model of liturgical prayer was, broadly speaking, formed of brief services characterized by frequent repetition of shorter passages of Scripture and increasingly by liturgical ceremonies such as the lighting of lamps, the offering of incense and so on. It suited those who were pursuing a life of prayer within a more secular environment. For considerably more scholarly and informed conversation on the development of early forms of Christian prayer, please see some of the recommended further reading.

What I would like to propose is that there are useful parallels which can be drawn between this model of desert and city in terms of the development of Christian prayer and our ecclesiological conversation. It would of course be ridiculous to overlay the model without modification but I believe there are some deeper truths to be gleaned. There is something about the rural rhythm of life, prayer and ministry, coupled with the distinctive geographical and sociological context we have already discussed, which lends itself to something of the 'desert' model of prayer and worship. There are strands of endurance and permanence which can be drawn on. How would it change our praying in rural communities if we made a little more explicit our intention to provide to the church in general an undergirding of prayer and praise, seeing that as part of the distinctive calling of church in the countryside? In the collection *Resourcing Rural Ministry: Practical Insights for Mission*, precisely this parallel is identified:

Norris describes how, in a monastic community, 'prayer rolls on, as daily as marriage and washing dishes'. This is a good description of worship in many small, rural churches. There are regular worshippers, who make up the visible body of Christ week by week, but there are also those in the local community who rarely participate in services and yet have a strong sense of belonging to 'our church' ... Rural worship is, for the most part, ordinary, yet particular because it is connected to its local context. (Hewlett in Martin, p. 85)

I do not claim that Hewlett was making precisely the connection that I am trying to make here, but the identification with the daily, weekly and yearly faithful round of prayer in a cloistered setting with the steady, perhaps unexciting, but faithful offering of praise and prayer by rural communities leads me to propose the interesting possibility of the rural church being a sort of dispersed collection of religious communities, each offering a vital, consistent and reliable ministry of prayer. What might it add to our rural ecclesiology if each little village, each small church and its diminutive congregation was seen as a cell, not only in terms of the cell church model of living cells in a body, but also of the stone cells in a monastery: each an individual powerhouse of sustained prayer, clustered around the cloister of a united benefice, group or deanery, in the same way that the individual cells of each monk or nun are sited around the cloister of an abbey or priory? Suddenly each rural church becomes an integral part of an endeavour which is distinct and exciting: the offering of daily prayer for the Church and the world, in a way that is contextually grounded, and, more than that, desperately needed.

I see other bits of the jigsaw falling into place when I reflect on the monastic model alongside the cell church model. The traditional offering of daily prayer in a Benedictine monastery is almost entirely non-Eucharistic. A literal following of the Rule of St Benedict would see the community joining together in prayer eight or nine times a day. One of those might be for the Eucharist, but the other occasions are all what we might now refer to as Services of the Word: Vigils, Prime, Lauds,

Tierce, Sext, Nones, Vespers and Compline. The vast majority of the diet of a religious community is the recitation of and reflection upon Scripture, either publicly in the Daily Offices or privately in study and *Lectio Divina*. If we were to offer this kind of model of prayer to the rural ministry of the Church of England, not over the course of one day, but perhaps over the course of a monthly service rota, we might find an engaging argument for a deepening of a pattern of worship based around familiar non-Eucharistic worship offered regularly at a predictable time every Sunday, with less of an emphasis placed on the importance of the weekly Eucharist. None of what I have just suggested is intended to devalue the offering of the Eucharist; quite the reverse. There may well be rural parishes in which a weekly, or even daily, offering of the Eucharist is sustainable, welcome and life changing. What I am suggesting, however, is that if we build an ecclesiology of rural ministry which identifies the individual cell of the body as essential and identifies each individual church as something like a stone cell or room within a monastery, what begins to emerge is quite an exciting model of multi-parochial benefices as organisms consisting of multiple parts, all of which are committed to sustaining not only their own life, but the life of the church more generally, offering something like a monastic undergirding of the Christian endeavour in prayer. The vital elements of this model are the importance of every individual person and congregation within it and the regularity, predictability and sustainability of the offering.

Dow suggests that the vision of the 'royal priesthood' in the First Letter of Peter is a useful text in thinking about how a rural congregation prays (1 Peter 2.9). He sees each individual Christian and each distinct rural community as a channel sustaining the communication between heaven and earth:

The local Christians in any community are now God's priestly people; they are primary channels between heaven and earth for that community. From earth to heaven they offer worship to God, with intercession and cries for the needs of the people. From heaven to earth they are God's channels to bring the message of salvation, God's forgiveness, healing and blessing to the people where they live. This is both a wonderful calling and an enormous privilege for the local church; sadly, it is rarely understood as such. (Dow, pp. 24–5)

His point is valid for any Christian community, but its importance for sustaining a robust ecclesiology of rural church is profound.

6 We need to be confident about our strengths

The Church of England has a problem with confidence. Partly this is due to the frequent, but erroneous, assumption that confidence is the same as arrogance. There is no place in the Church for arrogance. Confidence, on the other hand, is an important theological virtue. Confidence springs from a recognition that God is in charge and we are not. Proper Christian confidence is always rooted in the Incarnation and the Resurrection, and takes seriously the promises of the God who says to us, 'Do not fear for I have redeemed you: I have called you by name, you are mine' (Isa. 43.1). Proper Christian confidence is humble, seeking to rely entirely on God. The world is unlikely to be captivated by a Christianity which is presented apologetically, half-heartedly or with a hint of embarrassment; whereas a quiet, humble but confident faith has the potential to be attractive.

A quiet, humble but confident rural expression of faith is going to be contextual, just as our honesty about our weaknesses will likewise be contextual. Rural churches will do well to have a rational and realistic appraisal of their relative strengths and weaknesses, something a bit like a SWOT test, never forgetting that all strengths are God-given and all weaknesses contain an opportunity for growth as well. Lack, to whom I have already referred, notes:

There are two common fallacies about rural worship:
• with such small numbers you simply cannot have worship that lifts the spirit.

- the small rural church could worship like a town church, if only it got its act together.

Neither is true. Rural worship can have extraordinary immediacy and power, as well as intimacy. But it is true that some rural churches do not play to their strengths, or reach their potential. (Lack, p. 3)

Here I think Lack offers three crucial strengths of the rural church: immediacy, power and intimacy. All three manifest themselves out of the particular geographical and sociological context which we have already discussed and are made concrete in terms of the type of community in which the rural church ministers. Smaller communities offer an immediacy which is distinct. The physical presence of a large building in a small community projects something about the power of God (though again we need to be careful with the language of power and ensure that it is confidence and not arrogance we're talking about) and the comparatively small congregations, communities and interlocking social groups offer the distinct ecclesiological intimacy we have already discussed in our conversation about cell church and monasticism.

Having asserted the theology, practical strengths then follow. Several useful reviews of the strengths of rural communities have been published over the last decade, among which Dow provides a useful list:

- Rural society is deeply pastoral.
- In rural settings the church community cannot easily be distinguished from the wider local community.
- The church building is valued … it is a sign of God's presence.
- Numbers attending church are far higher than in urban areas.
- There are Church of England schools. (Dow, pp. 3–4, 12)

These are fair observations. Dow unpacks these points in more detail, noting that in regard to his penultimate point he is talking about percentages of the population attending church, not raw figures! Lack makes a similar observation, where he cites a 20% attendance at Christmas, as compared to 4% attendance of the population as a national average (Lack, p. 23). These figures were accurate as of 2008, although I suspect the percentages have not changed that much in the past decade, whereas the raw data may well have done so.

Dow's final point is among his most important. One of the extraordinary strengths of the rural church are its schools. I do not believe their importance can be overstated. The relative distribution of schools, particularly primary schools, through rural England provides another set of 'seeds in holy ground'. Moreover, the relationship between the rural church and schools has historically been excellent. The vast majority of my parochial experience, working with both Church of England and community schools, has been to find the door almost always at least half open. The vicar, and by extension other representatives of the local church, are often a fixture of school life, offering assemblies, 'Open the Book', listening to children reading and very often providing the venue for carol services, harvest festivals and fêtes. One of the interesting dynamics in a rural context is that it is entirely possible that the largest congregation to worship in any given week is quite likely to be in the local school rather than in the church. Certainly this was true in the Severnside Benefice where I took a weekly Monday morning assembly in the local Church of England primary school and a monthly assembly in the local community school (see Figure 2, p. xxix). Both schools were small, with numbers on roll of about 150, but this meant that on a Monday morning I conducted worship for a congregation which was probably 10 times larger than any of my Sunday congregations. Moreover, 90% of the congregation were under 12 years old! Looking back now, I often wonder why I didn't think to register these acts of worship in the parish registers. It would have made a profound difference to my Statistics for Mission returns each year!

Where appropriate and possible, with good relationships between local ministers, the Head Teacher and the PCC, the local schools find their place within that developing ecclesiological map as vital and integral centres of prayer, worship and ministry. The assembly hall becomes a chapel, just like the other buildings, and in quite a few cases the Monday morning assembly (or equivalent) becomes the principal act of worship of the week, around which the other Sunday and midweek congregations gather like monastic cells around the cloister.

7 We need to be honest about our weaknesses

Dow provided us with a useful set of strengths to frame our thinking, and he also provides a set of comparative weaknesses, which might be a good place for us to start:

- Silence on spiritual matters is normal.
- Those who farm are very busy.
- The church buildings are designed for congregations much larger than the normal weekly congregation.
- The age profile of the congregation does not give rise to optimism.
- Church is seen as for women and those who have retired.
- Multi-parish benefices are tiring and difficult to manage. (Dow, pp. 4–5)

Again these observations are inevitably generalizations and we might take issue with one or more of them in our particular context. I suspect, however, that most rural ministers will, like me, recognize a lot of truth in the list. In both the rural contexts in which I have ministered for a prolonged period, these aspects of ministry have been evident. The reality of 'managing' a multi-parochial benefice is both time-consuming and difficult. I have worked in a suburban context, as a residentiary canon in a busy cathedral, and am now self-employed, but I have never been more tired, or worked more hours in the average week, than when I was a rural vicar. There is something about the multiplication of tasks, meetings and acts of worship that simply costs more in terms of time and energy. In what follows in this book we will therefore take this aspect of rural ministry very seriously. The aim of this book is not to increase the workload on the rural priest, PCC or ministry team, but rather to help these people to lead their people into deeper and more sustained prayer. It is important to say at this point, however, that everything we discuss in the rest of this volume is going to have the practical realities of rural ministry firmly in its consciousness.

I want to take heart that in the main, Dow's list of 'weaknesses' are broadly practical in nature: they concern the physical plant, the number of potential worshippers, the practical realities of pastoring four, six or a dozen discrete communities. In contrast, if you cast your eyes back to Dow's list of strengths, they are broadly ecclesiological. In other words, the strengths have a spiritual or theological dimension to them which the weaknesses do not share. That is encouraging, and the right way around! It doesn't make the weaknesses any easier to resolve in the short term, but hopefully what it does is place them in a theological framework within which we can begin to build an understanding of the rural context. It is also true to say that there are aspects of almost all the weaknesses we have identified that could potentially be strengths, and vice versa. A lot of the literature written around rural ministry tacitly acknowledges this without necessarily spelling it out. Small congregations, as one example, are both strength and weakness: even the minister who works in a bustling cathedral with four or five hundred communicants at the main Sunday service will recognize that there is something particular and wonderful about the quiet midweek Eucharist to which only a handful of people come. The difference, of course, is that in a cathedral one has the best of both worlds, whereas in rural ministry very often the small congregation is the only congregation.

We are drawing near to the end of this first chapter, where we have sought to set out some key ecclesiological aspects of rural ministry. What we will do in the next chapter is to complement those with some liturgical theology which will form the basis of the three more practical chapters that follow. It is vital to have our ecclesiology and liturgical theology uppermost in our minds when we begin to consider the practical outworking of planning and leading worship in rural ministry.

This book is going to proceed on the assumption that the very heart of what we do is that we pray. The healthiest churches are those which pray and when churches thrive, it is usually also because they are praying hard. The next chapter will therefore pick up where this one leaves off, and consider what we might want to say about why and how the church prays. I will want to point again to some useful aspects of both Dow and Lack's work, but also to begin to challenge some of their assumptions.

Joining the threads

We carry forward into our conversation about liturgical theology some principles about the ecclesiology of rural ministry. We began by stating two key principles: first, that God is eternal and unchanging and second, that our experience and interaction with that eternal and unchanging God is contextual. These twin assertions led us to identify that the proper first step in considering rural mission and ministry is to consider what a distinctly rural ecclesiology might look like. We noted that rural churches and rural communities are distinctive. We recognized this is to do with physical geography, the social geography of our communities, and that small rural churches are not failed large churches. They have something distinctive and significant to say to their communities and the Church at large. In trying to identify what that distinctive and significant offering might be we drew on both the model of cell church and the example of Religious communities. We considered the way in which a sustained life of prayer based on small praying communities might offer something useful to our understanding of the rural church and potentially crystallize a distinctive vocational call upon the rural church which might be offered for the entire Church. We tried to be confident about the strengths of the rural church, as well as being honest about the potential weaknesses. We drew hope from the fact that while the weaknesses have a tendency to be more practical in nature, we can identify many of the positives as deeply theological. We now carry that learning forward into a conversation more specifically focused upon worship.

2

Our Duty and Our Joy: Liturgical Theology for the Rural Church

Starting properly

Thomas Merton, the renowned Cistercian monk and spiritual writer of the twentieth century, writes of a fledgling Cistercian community, Our Lady of the Valley, in Rhode Island in the early years of the twentieth century. According to his account the community was not growing, was not attracting people to ask for admittance as postulants. There was a great deal of activity going on, with particular attention paid to the fabric of the buildings, to agriculture and so on, but Merton notes that the eventual flourishing of this community was, in fact, down to something very different indeed:

> One solution to all the difficulties of the Valley, the one thing which turned it from a failure into a success, should, after all, have been obvious. Perhaps the founders had not reasoned out their problems with the logic of the first Cistercians. They had thought material success was necessary before they could hope to be truly contemplative. They apparently believed that they would be able to give all the required time to prayer only when they had grown into a big, solid community with many novices. Actually, it was just the other way round. The reason that they had no novices was precisely that they were not truly contemplatives. The reason they had such a struggle was that they could not give themselves entirely to the life of prayer that was required of them. (Merton, p. 180)

Merton, a contemplative monk, is clear that for any contemplative community to succeed, the bedrock of prayer must be established as absolutely paramount. On that bedrock the ministry of the local Christian community can be established. His example concerns an explicitly Religious community, and Merton is an avowed advocate of the contemplative life, but his point is easily transferable to any Christian community. The parallels with the parable of the wise and foolish man are also obvious (Matt. 7.24–27). Starting properly in any Christian endeavour is essential and for any Christian, whether individual or community, the proper place to start is conversation with God. The simplest definition of 'prayer' is precisely that: conversation with God.

This book is about a set of specific liturgical opportunities: the Christmas and Easter cycles and the distinctly agricultural festivals. Chapters 3, 4 and 5 will focus on the opportunities and challenges presented by these high points in the Christian year. It would be remiss, however, to begin there, without doing two things first: to say something about the primacy of prayer and to get our liturgical theology straight in our head.

The primacy of prayer

In the story of the monastery of Our Lady of the Valley, we are offered an example of one of the easiest and most common traps that any parish priest, indeed any Christian, falls into: the trap of forgetting to say our prayers. It is the easiest thing in the world to separate our diary commitments into two different categories: optional and compulsory, or, as I prefer, 'soft' and 'hard'. The 'hard' items in our daily diary are those to which we feel the most obligation to commit, perhaps because they are public and people will notice if we are not there, or perhaps because we instinctively enjoy them more. Maybe other people have imposed an obligation on us to consider those things to be the highest priority. For whatever reason, these are the ones that we are least willing to allow to slide. In contrast, the 'soft' diary items in the schedule of a parish priest, particularly a rural one (at least in my experience), are those things which few people will notice if we do not fulfil. When I go to see my confessor, I regularly note that family time tends to fall into this 'soft' category: only my wife will notice if I work until 11 o'clock at night and don't stop for supper and a conversation, or if I cancel another date night. Some readers might recognize this pattern. Certainly for me, and I suspect for many of us, sustaining the regular round of daily prayer often gets mis-filed in the 'soft' category. Perhaps we inherit a parish where there has not been a recent tradition of public daily Offices, or where such services are advertised but no congregation regularly attends. It is enormously easy to allow this daily obligation to become something we do if we have time, or indeed to allow it to drop completely out of the list of priorities. We stop praying and we neglect the one thing which is the powerhouse of any Christian community and the duty and joy of the pastor of any parish.

I use the term 'duty and joy' advisedly. Addressing the 'duty' part first, it is instructive that when we study *The Canons of the Church of England*, we notice that daily prayer crops up several times. It is mentioned in Canon B11, which is interested in the daily routine of the parish, and mentioned again in Canons C24 and C26 which focus on the life of the minister. When the Canons repeat things, it is usually a clue there is something deeply important at the root of the repetition. What the Church of England is trying to say by codifying the importance of daily prayer is this: it is of absolute importance to the individual minister, but not only that, it is also of absolute importance to the *community*.

A brief recap of the Canons is worth our time. First, we note that a life of prayer and study is considered essential for all ordained persons:

Every clerk in Holy Orders is under obligation, not being let by sickness or some other urgent cause, to say daily the Morning and Evening Prayer, either privately or openly; and to celebrate the Holy Communion, or be present thereat, on all Sundays and other principal Feast Days ... to be diligent

in daily prayer and intercession, in examination of … con-
science, and in the study of the Holy Scriptures … (Canon
C26.1)

As a reassurance, the sections omitted and marked by ellipses
are not substantial edits, but merely an attempt to remove the
exclusive language which, almost unbelievably, still exists even
in the online text. We note that this obligation includes daily
recitation of morning and evening prayer and regular reception
of Holy Communion, together with personal prayer, intercession, confession and study of the Scriptures. This is no less
than an obligation to a balanced and rigorous spiritual life.
The Church of England requires its clergy to be people who
are grounded in prayer, Bible reading and study. It is this that
will resource and release them into the rest of their ministry. As
an aside, we note that this obligation is on *all* ordained people,
without distinction in terms of appointment, stipendiary or
not, retired or not. I am now a retired priest with permission
to officiate and I find myself under exactly the same obligation
as the full-time stipendiary priest who has taken over from me
in my last paid post. It is an obligation because the Church
knows that it matters. It matters because the Christian who
prays becomes a Christian through whom God moves.

Lest this chapter should begin to seem overly clerical, we
will turn our attention to Canon B11 before concluding this
section:

On all other days [than Sundays, which are dealt with in the
preceding Canon], the minister who has the cure of souls,
together with other ministers licensed to serve in the benefice
(or one or more of the benefices), shall make such provision
for Morning and Evening Prayer to be said or sung either in
at least one of the churches in the benefice (or at least one of
the churches in at least one of the benefices) or, after con-
sultation with the parochial church council of each parish in
the benefice (or benefices), elsewhere as may best serve to sustain the corporate spiritual life of the benefice (or benefices)
and the pattern of life enjoined upon ministers by Canon

C26. Public notice shall be given by tolling the bell or other appropriate means, of the time and place where the prayers are to be said or sung. (Canon B11.2)

Far from the Church identifying daily prayer as something peculiar to her ordained clergy, here in Canon B11 we are reminded that daily prayer is at the heart of the life of the *community*. If we drill down into the substance of the Canon, navigating our way through the multiple sets of brackets and subclauses, we learn that the leader of any Christian community has an obligation to provide daily prayer which is corporate, regular, accessible and public. Yes, the obligation falls only on the clergy and licensed lay ministers to actually attend, but the spirit of this piece of important ecclesiology is that everyone in the community should know that the very framework of ministry among them is prayer, and there should be a real effort made to sustain that prayer in a way which is predictable (so people know they can turn up if they want to), accessible (which is what the clause about the venue for daily prayer is getting at) and public, hence the ringing of the church bell. Once again, I am reassured by this Canon, because not only does it stress the importance of regular prayer, but it is also willing for the local community to ascertain the how, when and where. In other words, here is the Church of England being *contextual*. We recognize the recurring pattern of something non-negotiable being, at the same time, utterly contextual. Pray we must. How, when and where are properly local decisions.

One obvious example of contextualization is the permission to pray somewhere other than the church building. Of course the church building is, in theory, exactly the right place to say our daily prayers. It ought to be the default, which is why the Canon starts from there. That model of regular prayer in the representative building builds upon our ecclesiology of the visible, incarnational church. It is also good for our churches to be prayed in: buildings absorb prayer and gain character from that process. There may well, however, be good reasons not to pray in the church building all the time. If our church building is miles away from every population centre, which is not unusual in some rural parishes, or so unbelievably expensive to heat in winter that to pray in it would be either fiscally imprudent or perishingly uncomfortable, then we are to be wise and choose somewhere else. That might be the vicarage study, or the conference room of the local primary school, or the coffee shop. The point is that we still pray, and we do so in a publicly accessible place that is advertised, and to which people are alerted. It is interesting that over the months of lockdown my Facebook and YouTube feeds have become overwhelmed by notifications telling me that Christian communities whom I 'follow' are about to begin their morning or evening prayers. I have prayed with communities all over the country, and further abroad, in real time and the requirement to toll the bell has been fulfilled by the pinging of my iPad notifications!

Before moving on to the more complicated and high-profile liturgies of the liturgical year, I strongly encourage every minister and congregation to consider, revisit, and perhaps explore with the PCC, the routine, regular offering of prayer within the parish. It is something that is neglected too often and which cannot but lead to spiritual malaise. We are in an age where we naturally baulk at language of obligation, but we ought to revisit why the Church would lay such an obligation upon her people. It is, surely, because time and experience has proven that where prayer is regular, faithful, corporate, accessible and public, the kingdom grows. We will each have other obligations on our lives, perhaps particularly of family, secular employment or illness, which will tempt us to slacken, or omit entirely, the 'soft' aspects of our daily diary, which too often includes morning and evening prayer. We need to resist that temptation. There is always a way to flex our diary to allow us the 30 minutes or so in 24 hours to hold ourselves, our loved ones, our community and our church before God and allow him to love us, and them, into the kingdom. Other things might have to give way. Some of those things might need to be negotiated with the PCC, or with colleagues, or with the family. We might need to be imaginative with timings. We might need to rely on our colleagues a little more. We might need to be willing to be very practical. Some of our models might be quite radically different to how they were before the 2020 pandemic and might well include considerably more streamed and webcast content. We may very well be tolling the bell by email or social media as well as physically. But we must make sure that the basics are sorted. We have to pray. It is an obligation for a reason.

I remember about a year into my first incumbency, I turned up at my spiritual director's house just before Christmas and moaned at him that Morning and Evening Prayer were a misery because my church was stone cold, and although I rang the bell no one came. His advice to me was blisteringly practical: 'Pray faster, Tom!' I did, and having my resolve sharpened by a piece of blunt honesty from a trusted colleague helped me to turn a corner in my attitude to daily prayer in that context. I adjusted the time slightly, and preached more about it, and actually within a year or so I was being joined by laypeople from a couple of the villages. Less than a year on from my grumpy rant to my spiritual director, I was being summoned to prayer by a parishioner who had got to church before me ringing the bell!

Liturgy as the heartbeat of the rural church

At the beginning of Chapter 1, we noted that all our thinking about worship is framed by two truths: God is eternal and we are contextual. That helped us to build up an ecclesiology of the rural Church of England. In the same way we were able to do that, so too we must be able to develop a theological understanding of the Church's liturgy which takes our obligation to pray very seriously and also helps us to develop that pattern of prayer in a way which is sane, sensible and appropriate to the context in which God has placed us. We have just reminded ourselves that prayer is vital and that without it our other endeavours are unlikely to succeed. We now need to consider how we do that praying where we are.

Michael Perham, an architect of *Common Worship* and one-time Bishop of Gloucester, defined liturgy as 'that subtle blend of word, song, movement, gesture and silence that enables the people of God to worship together' (Perham, p. 3). Liturgy, then, includes not only words but the silences between them, the options and freedoms afforded us by the notes and rubrics, singing, symbols, postures and also the physical aids to worship that surround us, perhaps most chiefly including our buildings. As we build a model for doing liturgical theology in rural communities, we will need to hold in our minds that we are not only talking about dealing with text. We are talking about creating corporate worship which takes seriously not only the words we use, but also all those other facets mentioned by Perham that come together to constitute an act of worship. When we are talking about multi-parochial rural worship, we will need to take the worshipping context seriously. The remainder of this book will consider three particular instances where the rural ministry team has to make decisions about where, when and how acts of worship will take place. Which building we use is a liturgical decision as well as a pastoral one. Some worship spaces might lend themselves more easily to a particular liturgy. Proximity to a school might make a significant difference to the sort of congregation we might gather, particularly for services taking place during term time.

We have said earlier that there is something distinctly incarnational about doing ecclesiology. We are paying attention to the way in which the church is, by its very nature, rooted in a particular community, in a particular society, at a particular time. What we are now attempting to do is to connect that incarnational model of church with the great story of redemption, of salvation, the resurrection of our Lord from the dead, which it is the primary purpose of the liturgy to communicate. The ordination service reminds the candidate for the priesthood that chief among the tasks of priest and people is, 'with all God's people ... to tell the story of God's love' (CW: OS, p. 37). The story of God's love is the story of the life, death and resurrection of Jesus Christ which wrought for us our salvation. That great Easter story is eternal, glorious and transcendent. It is that story that the liturgy tells, in the daily, weekly and yearly cycles of the seasons of the Christian year.

Day in and day out we proclaim, 'Christ has died! Christ is risen! Christ will come again!' Above all this is an Easter message. And just as Christmas and Easter are wonderfully and eternally linked, so our local worship, incarnational in nature because it is rooted in the particular, communicates the eternal and unending truths of salvation wrought for us in the darkness between Good Friday and Easter morning.

It is reassuring that this recognition of the vital importance of the regular telling of the story of redemption through public worship is acknowledged by theologians from across the spectrum of church style and denomination. Here is Elliott, describing the centrality of the liturgical cycle in a liturgical manual of the Roman Catholic Church:

> Christians understand time differently from other people because of the liturgical year. We are drawn into a cycle that becomes such a part of our lives that it determines how we understand the structure of each passing year. In the mind of the Christian, each passing year takes the shape, not so much around the cycle of natural seasons, the financial or sporting year or academic semesters, but around the feasts, fasts and seasons of the Catholic Church. Without thinking much about it, from early childhood, we gradually learn to see time itself, past, present and future, in a new way. All of the great moments of the liturgical year look back to the salvific events of Jesus Christ, the Lord of history. Those events are made present here and now as offers of grace, yet they bear strong pre-sentiments of eternity. (Elliott, p. 1)

In the final line of that rather splendid quotation, Elliott explicitly notes the 'eternal' events which are being made present in our particular context, in our particular time. The local community, by claiming the saving acts of God 'in season and out of season' (CW: OS, p. 37, based on 2 Tim. 4.2) takes its place as a vital part of the entire worshipping Church.

The more evangelical approach of Dow, which we have already considered in Chapter 1, begins from a different place but puts the same primacy on acts of worship. Dow develops a model for ministry based on Ephesians 4 and identifies the five 'major ministries' of pastor, apostle, prophet, evangelist and teacher. It is the role of pastor that Dow identifies as the most vital and for Dow that is because the pastor is intimately connected to worship. He notes, 'rural communities are instinctively pastoral. If a minister is not pastoral their message cannot be heard', and although in a rural community the other four ministries do not necessarily have to be resident, 'the pastor ... must normally be present when the people gather for worship or fellowship and they must be easily accessible throughout the week' (Dow, p. 6). While there is much in Dow with which I do not agree, it is instructive that the necessity for sustained, intimate and regular local acts of worship are at the very top of the priority list in his model. He thus argues strongly against the type of 'rotational' rotas in rural areas where the time of the service and the person leading the local community in their worship, changes from week to week. Dow, just like Elliott, identifies the primacy of worship as the place where the family of God is constituted.

It is useful to hold these two examples together, because they remind us that the centrality of worship is not something that belongs to a particular church style or tradition. While there will be elements of both writers with which we might disagree when it comes to specific outworking of their models, we move forward clear in our minds that establishing public worship, liturgy, is essential for the flourishing of any church. When we consider rural communities there are some real challenges, as well as opportunities, many of which are peculiar to the agrarian context.

Family likeness: local expression

The Church of England supposes, and indeed encourages, local interpretation. One useful piece of evidence of this statement is the preface to the annual Lectionary booklet. You may well have one of these annual, disposable booklets in front of you. When one reads through the notes to the Lectionary, it becomes clear there are a number of aspects of family likeness which the Church expects all parishes and communities to observe: principally the Sunday Lectionary during the 'closed' seasons centred around Christmas and Easter, and the Principal Feasts and Festivals, which 'are not usually displaced' (CW: Lectionary, p. 6). By contrast, there is a whole section on 'Local Celebrations' where the local congregation is positively encouraged to identify key saints and other significant observations and give them prominence. Likewise, the 'minister' (by which I think in most circumstances we would include a local ministry team or PCC and the prevailing tradition of the parish) is encouraged to be selective about which Lesser Festivals or Commemorations might be appropriate in the local context. One worshipping community might make a decision to make full use of every Feast, Lesser Festival and Commemoration provided for in the Lectionary, together with appropriate observation of locally significant days and people, whereas another parish may well opt to observe almost no Feast days except for those Festivals identified as for universal observation. This is just one example of the way in which the Church of England not only gives permission, but actively encourages diversity and local practice that honours the tradition and history of our church, but also takes the local seriously. As it happens, I am writing this chapter on the 17th Sunday after Trinity in the year 2020, which happens to be 4 October. In the universal calendar, the Lesser Festival of St Francis of Assisi simply disappears in such a year, the Sunday taking priority. For communities with a particular link to St Francis, the option is provided in the Lectionary to 'upgrade' Francis to the status of a Festival and then observe his day on Sunday, in preference to Trinity 17. I could imagine, and indeed I have myself encouraged, a rural community to consider that their agricultural heartbeat is precisely the sort of local context in which this prioritizing of St Francis would be absolutely appropriate. Taking the opportunity to celebrate a saint whose popular tradition includes a particular care for the natural creation and animals ties in particularly strongly with such a community and may well enhance any observation of

Harvest Thanksgiving. We will return to this specific instance in Chapter 5. The point is made, however, that codified into what might appear to be a complex set of rules designed to inhibit freedom of expression is actually exactly the opposite: the positive encouragement to be local.

A liturgical theology for the rural church

We have remembered the principles we developed in Chapter 1 and identified how a parallel set of principles help us to shape our liturgical theology. I now outline a suggested model for doing liturgical theology in the church, which might be particularly helpful for rural ministry teams because it provides a method for identifying the key pieces of the story to be proclaimed liturgically where delivering the liturgical provision is challenging due to context. The model is applicable to any liturgical context, but will be most helpful where a number of decisions need to be made for practical as well as ecclesiological reasons. The model will be outlined here and has informed my prioritization of the various aspects considered in each of the succeeding chapters.

The principle is to take each liturgical celebration and examine it through three lenses: liturgical text, liturgical action and theological truth. I believe that by using this model, it will help the local liturgical practitioner to make sense of the wealth of provision that now exists, and to make decisions of principle and practice for the local community based on rigorously theological criteria. The matrix I propose for this model is in Figure 3.

Liturgical celebration	Liturgical text(s)	Liturgical action(s)	Theological truth

Figure 3: Liturgical Analysis Matrix

The use of an actual table is entirely optional but might appeal to people with minds like mine that naturally looks for lists, charts and diagrams! A local ministry team might just as easily take this model and use it for discussion around the PCC or worship committee table. Similarly, the specific titles of each column in the table are not set in stone but rather indicate the three lenses through which each liturgical celebration is examined. I will address each of the column headings briefly below.

Liturgical celebration

Remember this book is intended to be inherently practical. As I write the text, I imagine a vicar, PCC or ministry team trying to work out how to provide worship in their rural community. My proposal therefore is to start by examining the liturgical occasions we either must, or instinctively need, to make provision for. This book has identified what I believe to be the three vital instances: Christmas, Easter and the Agricultural Feasts. The following three chapters will be a practical outworking of this model for the liturgical theology focused on those three sets of feasts. There will be others, however, and the model works just as well for them. Suggestions for other occasions might include All Souls Day/Commemoration of the Faithful Departed. This is an occasion which, although developing out of a confidently Catholic tradition, has become much more widespread in recent years and speaks to a profound pastoral need in very many communities of allowing the bereaved to hold their grief somewhere safe into which the gospel can speak. Another example might be Mothering Sunday, which although it falls within the broader 'Easter cycle', has a distinct and honoured history and pastoral purpose of its own. A third example might be how to commemorate the patronal festivals of the local churches, which itself becomes complicated and burdensome when one has a multi-parochial benefice of perhaps 10 or 12 buildings, and no duplicated patronal saints! There may be specific pastoral events which could be analysed using the same model: for example, services to which those who have been baptized in recent years are invited back, or similar events for wedding couples.

The heading 'Liturgical Celebration' is a broad one, under which you can list any, and all, of the 'occasions' which might make up the liturgical year in your context. I encourage any local community to think imaginatively and comprehensively about what they might be, and then allow the model to draw out the theological and liturgical principles that will guide your observation of those occasions.

Liturgical text(s)

Queen among all liturgical texts is, of course, Scripture. The model therefore encourages beginning with the Bible readings. Even that is easier said than done because when we pick up our copy of the Lectionary again, we notice that for any day of the year, there are at least three sets of readings provided, plus additional options on many occasions. Zeroing in on the key biblical texts is a vital part of this model because it is from Scripture that we glean, in the words of the ordination service, 'all things necessary for eternal salvation through faith in Jesus Christ' (CW: OS, p. 16). Anglican liturgy has always been uncompromising in its expectation that we always begin with the Bible. Indeed, if we analyse any Church of England liturgy, any act of worship, the vast majority of the text is direct quotation from the Bible. The golden examples of this are Morning and Evening Prayer from the BCP which are almost entirely comprised of scriptural texts, before we even consider the significant portions of Scripture appointed for readings. Spending time looking at the Scripture readings suggested for the liturgical occasion in question is an excellent practice in its own right, and in some contexts beginning a meeting which is going to look at, for example, All Souls Day with a Bible study or a session of *lectio divina* might be an excellent way of focusing the ensuing discussion. Whenever we read the Scriptures, the Spirit moves!

Liturgical text also includes the liturgies themselves. Gone are the days, and broadly this is to be celebrated, where the only provision for a worshipping community was the BCP. The challenge now is that there is such a wealth of liturgical provision, including the BCP but also CW in its numerous volumes and the official or semi-official additional resource books that are frequently published which focus either on a particular season or a particular demographic within the worshipping community. There is a smorgasbord of provision, which can give us a feeling of liturgical indigestion. While no community is likely to make use of all the dozens of options, for the multi-parochial benefice, the sense of indigestion can be even more profound. I certainly recall sitting at my desk in the vicarage study with a sense of mounting panic as I looked at the volumes on my shelf and the emails issuing forth from Church House Westminster or the local diocesan office encouraging me to look at yet more new material. There needs to be some thoughtful sifting and selecting and this process of liturgical analysis will help us to do that.

The principle is to sit with the material until, being aware of it, we can discern where the core of the message is pointing us as a local community. We enter into this analysis with the expectation that we will definitely not be using all the material and asking the Spirit to aid us in wise judgement.

As mentioned above, liturgical text includes the notes, rubrics and appendices as well as the main texts. It is characteristic of CW in particular that often some of the flexibility and permissiveness only becomes apparent when we read all of the notes. This is regrettable, but unlikely to change, and so an exploration of all the provision is vital. Doing this early, and ideally corporately, can turn what might seem a tedious reading task into an imaginative and prayerful discernment process among colleagues.

Liturgical action(s)

Liturgical action refers to all the ceremonial, the visual, the participatory and everything else that falls under the important umbrella of 'action'. CW has always been very clear that a balanced act of worship must contain proportional amounts of 'word, prayer, praise and action' (*New Patterns for Worship* (NPW), p. 15). Liturgical action can be as simple but profound as the congregation standing for a reading from the Gospel – which reaches its pinnacle of profundity on Palm Sunday and Good Friday – or as involved and choreographed as a piece of liturgical dance, a procession of the Blessed Sacrament or a dramatic presentation of a reading with props, costumes and a large cast. NPW notes:

> Dramatic action might interpret the Word, or a procession or dance might help to express praise. So something might be done with music, or followed by silence, or accompanied by visuals, gestures or symbols. There might be a movement by the congregation, such as standing or joining hands, movement with an object, e.g. a candle or Bible, a change in lighting or visual presentation … The action may be the climax towards which the service moves, or an action that begins the worship and sets the theme for it. (NPW, p. 17)

As we read through liturgical text, suggestions and options for liturgical action will present themselves. Some of these will be explicit, for example in the encouragement provided in *Common Worship: Times and Seasons* (CW: TS) for a dramatic presentation of the Passion Narrative during Holy Week or a Palm Sunday procession. Others will be implicit, such as whether we might be able to hold worship in one or more of our working farms during the month of 'Creationtide'.

All these potential actions need to be listed in the third column of the matrix and then choices made about which ones might be utilized when the analysis is complete. We need always to be aware there will be more potentially exciting, creative things to do than most communities will be able to handle without confusion or fatigue creeping in!

Theological truth

Reaching the fourth column of the matrix, we arrive at the place where we can begin to join the dots. Remembering that our principal reason for worshipping together as Christians is to 'tell the story of God's love', our purpose is to discern what the heart of the story we are being called to tell really is. There are two traps worshipping communities often fall into. The first is either only telling one part of the story over and over again; perhaps an over-emphasis on the Cross to the exclusion of the Resurrection, or very limited use of Scripture that only speaks a narrow selection of the Bible into the community. The second trap ensnares us when our worshipping diet becomes so clogged with imaginative ideas that the consistency and coherence of the story can become occluded.

Reading across the row, we can bring together the texts, both scriptural and liturgical, and the potential liturgical actions and, in a process of discernment, work out what the theological message is, or, to put it another way, what mystery of salvation it is, that this particular act of worship will tell. Having done the groundwork of looking at the texts and the actions, we then discern the key theological truth that the act of worship will proclaim. We can then go back across the matrix in the opposite direction, from right to left, and thin out the text selections until we are left with the right combination for our particular context. It is important to start from the left-hand side because this is the process of discernment that leads us to theological truth. The journey back from right to left is not a journey of discernment, but rather of practical liturgical selection.

A *worked example of the liturgical theology matrix*

To illustrate the potential of this model of liturgical theological analysis, in Figure 4 is the beginning of a matrix focusing on the marking of All Souls Day/Commemoration of the Faithful Departed.

This matrix is the result of me sitting down at my desk and doing liturgical theological analysis, imagining that I am still priest-in-charge of the Severnside Benefice as I knew it when I was incumbent. As can be seen, there is an awful lot of text and a good deal of choice that could be made about actions as well. As I sift through the material, both from CW itself, and from the other sources such as the guide by Kennedy, full details of which are in the bibliography, I discover there is a good deal of thinning out to do in order to make this occasion manageable and powerful for people in my parishes. I am helped in this by getting to the right-hand side of the matrix and seeing that there are a set of principal theological truths that appear, like a golden thread, through all the material. There are also some secondary truths about judgement which are important but which I decide, on this occasion, not to prioritize. Having identified those, I can then work back through the matrix selecting the texts and actions which are going to be the most appropriate in my context. The next version of the table therefore is inevitably messy as I prioritize things, and strike other things out, and looks something like Figure 5.

Figure 5 is quite chaotic, but you can see that as I pray and discern and get clear in my head what the main theological themes are in the texts this year, I am able to identify the options that are going to speak into that context most appropriately and also that the type of service that is going to work best will be a non-Eucharistic service at the weekend. I decide that the symbol of light is the most important one so I move away from ideas around the graveyard or the crematorium, though I file those away for future reference. I read in various places that people can either take their candles with them or perhaps put them into a sand tray in front of an icon or the altar. Because I am drawn to themes around the space needed

Liturgical celebration: Commemoration of the Faithful Departed/All Souls Day

Liturgical text(s)	*Liturgical action(s)*	*Theological truth*
BCP: nothing! Could draw on material from the funeral?	Read names aloud?	'… raise it up on the last day' (John 6.39).
Bible readings: Lamentations 3 Wisdom 3 Psalm 23 or 27 Romans 5 1 Peter 1 John 5 or John 6	Light candles? The people hold them? Do they take them home? Do they leave them in church?	The Resurrection is a promise. That promise is like a light in the dark place.
CW: TS	Prayer cards?	But…
A Eucharist? Not sure how many of our folk this would work for? Kennedy gives a non-Eucharistic structure	Should we do something in the graveyard?	Death is real and so is grief (1 Peter 1).
Commemoration of the Faithful Departed? In its printed form, or in the way Kennedy suggests?	What about something at the crematorium?	We need space to grieve (Psalm 23).
When? Sunday evening? The Praxis guide encourages this. 2 November?	Should we write to the bereaved? If so, how many years back?	There is judgement too (John 5).
What about the Thanksgiving or the Holy Ones of God? Has a nice bit at the end where you can make it local/personalize.		
Draw some material from CW: PS?		

Figure 4: Liturgical Analysis matrix – All Souls/Commemoration of the Faithful Departed

Liturgical celebration: Commemoration of the Faithful Departed/All Souls Day

Liturgical text(s)	_Liturgical action(s)_	_Theological truth_
Bible readings: Psalm 23 1 Peter 1 John 6	Read names aloud? _Not at main service._	** ' … raise it up on the last day' (John 6.39) ** _base sermon on this passage._
CW: TS	Light candles? _Yes_ The people hold them? Do they take them home? _Yes_	The Resurrection is a promise.
A Eucharist? Not sure how many of our folk this would work for? Kennedy gives a non-Eucharistic structure	~~Do they leave them in church?~~	That promise is like a light in the dark place.
Commemoration of the Faithful Departed? In its printed form,~~ or in the way Kennedy suggests?~~	Prayer cards? _Yes_	But…
When? Sunday evening? The Praxis guide encourages this. _Main service (non-Eucharistic)_	~~Should we do something in the graveyard?~~	Death is real and so is grief (1 Peter 1).
2 November? _Quiet evening Eucharist._	~~What about something at the crematorium?~~	We need space to grieve (Psalm 23).
What about the Thanksgiving or the Holy Ones of God? Has a nice bit at the end where you can make it local/personalize. _Use on 2 Nov_	Should we write to the bereaved? If so, how many years back?	~~There is judgement too (John 5)~~
~~Draw some material from CW: PS?~~		

Figure 5: Liturgical Analysis matrix – All Souls/Commemoration of the Faithful Departed – showing my workings!

for proper grieving (a theme that the First Letter of Peter has led me to), I decide that the congregation will take the candles with them and there will be an invitation to light them at home which I will include during the sermon. I decide that, in my context, one principal symbol is probably best so I will not have the names of the departed read out loud on this occasion, rather there will be profound silence during the commemoration while people can hold their lighted candles and offer the names that matter to them in silence.

As I continue to think, I am convinced by the fact that Holy Communion is a really important context for remembering the departed. I decide to offer a quiet Holy Communion service on 2 November itself and that I will make a list available at the end of the Sunday service where people can write down names if they would like me to mention them at that quieter service later in the week. I might use some of the Bible readings I didn't use on the Sunday at that secondary commemoration.

Having arrived at my set of decisions, I can tidy up my matrix to display the liturgical texts, liturgical actions and theological truths that my All Souls Day service this year will be framed around, as shown in Figure 6.

Liturgical celebration: Commemoration of the Faithful Departed/All Souls Day

Liturgical text(s)	Liturgical action(s)	Theological truth
Bible readings: Psalm 23 (hymn) 1 Peter 1 John 6		** '... raise it up on the last day' (John 6.39) ** base sermon on this passage.
Sunday evening Main service (non-Eucharistic) with Commemoration of the Faithful Departed in its printed form.	Invite everyone to whom we have ministered in the last three years. Light candles. The people hold them and then take them home.	The Resurrection is a promise. That promise is like a light in the dark place. But...
	Offer them a prayer card when they leave together with opportunity for the name to be read on 2 November.	Death is real and so is grief (1 Peter 1).
2 November Quiet evening Eucharist including reading of names and Thanksgiving or the Holy Ones of God. Wisdom 3 Romans 5 John 5	Read the names at this service.	We need space to grieve (Psalm 23).

Figure 6: Liturgical Analysis matrix – All Souls/Commemoration of the Faithful Departed – completed

48

Joining the threads

We have explored a potential way of sifting through the vast amounts of material the Church provides and identifying what might be appropriate within our context. The model I have outlined takes seriously what we discussed in Chapter 1 about our ecclesiology and the conversation at the beginning of this chapter about the primacy of prayer. It is a confidently Anglican model for liturgical theological analysis because it begins with Scripture and only then looks at the rest of the liturgical material. It is through a prayerful engagement with these primary and essential texts, which are then considered alongside our context and the variety of material available, that we are led to some theological truths that are what we are called to proclaim. Having started with the Scripture, and found doctrine, we can then make our decisions and begin planning our liturgies.

As I noted above, there is no requirement to actually use this matrix in the form in which I present it here. It will help some people, not others. The principles underlying it, however, are really important, because they hold us to our Anglican heritage, gather in all the traditional and newer resources and keep our eyes constantly fixed on the proclamation of the truths of the death and Resurrection of Jesus Christ. This way, we don't fall into the trap of accidentally beginning our planning from the point of sheer practicality rather than the Scripture and the worship of the Church. The practicalities are vital to address, and they are addressed, but in a healthy relationship to Scripture, liturgy, doctrine and, above all, Christ.

3

Advent and Christmas

Times and Seasons

The Church of England's book of resources for marking the liturgical year is, not without reason, called *Times and Seasons*. The reference is biblical, drawn from Daniel's response to his vision from God: 'Blessed be the name of God from age to age, for wisdom and power are his. He changes times and seasons, deposes kings and sets up kings' (Dan. 2.20–21). The rhythms and cycles of both the created world and the Church of God are fundamental to our worship. There is another important aspect we can draw from the title. There are *times*, and there are *seasons*. In other words the Christian year, in the same way as most secular calendars, consists of a certain number of fixed dates or occasions as well as longer periods of time called seasons. For example, there is a season of Christmas which could be 12 or possibly 40 days long but within that there is only one day which is Christmas Day: 25 December. The latter we might call a time, within the former which is a season. So there is an interlocking of seasonal time and date-specific time. One of the most obvious examples that most reasonably liturgical communities will encounter is the fact that the Feast of the Annunciation, fixed on 25 March, can fall within Lent or Eastertide, lending a distinct flavour to that celebration depending on when it happens to fall.

This is actually very helpful to have clear in our minds as we begin to consider the period of Advent and Christmas. Imagine yourself back in that meeting of the PCC or worship committee, looking at what worship might be offered during the winter in your community. Recognizing there are a certain number of fixed dates which will need to be resourced in some way, but that there are also broader periods of time with the seasonal flavour, can go a long way not only to making the provision of acts of worship manageable, but also to injecting some really creative seasonality into our offering.

One of the reasons for looking at Advent and Christmas first, and then moving on to Lent, Holy Week and Easter in the next chapter, is that the balance between times and seasons is rather different in each case. This impacts how we might structure opportunities for worship across a multi-parochial benefice, and it is something a lot of the more recent liturgical manuals don't pay very much attention to. Unlike Holy Week, which has a number of observations within it which have specific dates upon which they need to be celebrated (in this example, all calculated with reference to the date of Easter), the Advent and Christmas cycle has relatively few specific days which are immovable, and relatively more seasonal emphasis which allows for the story to be told in a slightly more flexible manner.

This chapter, and the two that follow it, will be structured in a similar way. First, we will make some ecclesiological observations about the nature of the season. We will then look through the lens of liturgical theology at the broad brush-strokes of the season. What I include in this section has been determined by undertaking some of the liturgical-theological analysis outlined in Chapter 2. This will hopefully inspire you to undertake some of this analysis for yourself, making use of the analytical matrix to see what emerges in your own context. We will then explore a few specific examples of how the season might be observed in a distinctly rural context.

A glance through the ecclesiological lens

The entire Christian experience is framed and understood by reference to the Incarnation and the Resurrection. Both are intimately linked, form the story of our salvation, and offer us insights into our faith in the place where God has called us to

worship him. Although it is in many ways a gross oversimplifi-
cation, it can be helpful to reflect on the Incarnation as saying
some important things about locality, groundedness and presence, and the Resurrection as reminding us of some important
truths about transcendence and eternity. Let me repeat that I
am not for a moment trying to separate these two mysteries of
our redemption, but simply pointing out we learn things from
both of them which are applicable to the conversation we are
having here.

With that in mind, the heart of the Christmas cycle is of
course the Incarnation. The Feast of the Nativity of Christ
on 25 December tells the story of God come down. There
is therefore something distinctively incarnational about the
whole of the season and that needs to be taken seriously. It
doesn't do to drive too much of a wedge between the 'popular' observance of Christmas, with its emphasis on celebration,
relationship, gift-giving and gathering in the family home,
and the religious observance. The emphases I've just listed
are all deeply layered into the story of Christmas which itself
is about a family beset with its own challenges and stresses,
seeking a location in which they can be safe as they respond
to a government initiative. The theme of home, or sanctuary,
is never far from the surface, from the domestic settings of
the Annunciation, or the Visitation of Mary to Elizabeth, to
the borrowed stable, or the flight into Egypt. I emphasize this
because I think it helps us to unpack why the local is so important in the observation of Christmas in rural communities. In
later sections we will explore some of the imaginative ways in
which services might move around different church buildings
in the parish or benefice and ways in which disparate congregations might be encouraged to join together for worship. My
instinct is that this is unlikely to be well received at Christmas.
Ecclesiologically speaking, there is a profound relationship
between people and their building which, other than perhaps
for the pastoral Offices, is probably at its peak at Christmas.
This has implications for the provision of worship on the 24
and 25 December in particular which, now that Epiphany
and Candlemas are permitted to be observed away from their

proper dates, is probably the main fixed point in the Christmas season. We are likely to be responding to a demand for a number of church services and events during this season and those clustered most closely around 25 December are likely to need to take place in the local church. This has implications for staffing and for service rotas.

The other principal locations for Christmas celebrations are also likely to be local and are probably the home and the school. There might also be other important local venues depending upon the demography and population of your community. The local pub, care home or hospital might become particularly prominent during the season of Christmas as places where liturgical, or para-liturgical, worship might take place. In the year 2020 in particular, due to ongoing restrictions in the midst of the coronavirus pandemic, the churchyard and other open spaces are already being identified as significant new gathering places. At the point of writing it is hard to know whether or not this will be an anomaly in 2020. In general terms, probably the home and the school are the most universal and will need careful consideration. The date of Christmas never changes, but of course the day of the week on which Christmas Day falls changes every year, which has a knock-on effect on how long the season of Advent is. Advent can be almost four full weeks, or only just three weeks, long. This is likely to mean the relationship of the end of school term to Christmas Day is also flexible. Finally, we are all aware that people's holiday patterns tend to change depending on when the end of term falls and when in the week Christmas falls. All of these are important factors to bear in mind when beginning to sketch out what any given Christmas season might look like. None of these variables are peculiar to the rural church, but patterns of behaviour and relationships are distinct, and those overlapping communities we discussed in Chapter 1 are likely to mean some careful consideration needs to be given to the relationship between Christmas celebrations in church buildings, in the school and in the home. A key ecclesiological question for the group planning the worship for this Christmas season is therefore going to be around where we 'find' Christmas in our local community. Where is Christmas 'located'? Which bits of the observance absolutely need to be very local, and which bits might lend themselves to cut a bit more of a geographical safari?

A glance through the liturgical-theological lens

The 'Christmas season' is a catch-all expression for the period of the Christian year which centres on the celebration of the Nativity of our Lord on 25 December. There are any number of liturgical manuals and commentaries on the liturgical year, some of which I provide details of, and it is not difficult to become lost in liturgical and historical analysis! I do not propose to duplicate much of that conversation here. It is worth noting, however, that this period of the year has been rather more elastic than its counterpart centred around Easter. What comprises the Christmas season, or Christmas cycle, has historically been flexible. This is a useful reminder that Christian practice develops over time and that it doesn't do to develop a rigidity which might stifle genuine Christian expression and worship. It is also a gift to rural Christianity, where very often there are too many communities and too many buildings to be able to deliver everything on a very small selection of dates.

To take a very general overview then, Christmas Day itself is preceded by a vigil, Christmas Eve and is followed by 12 days of celebration culminating in the Feast of the Epiphany on 6 January. That is the heart of the celebration from a liturgical point of view. To this 14-day celebration we can then add the season of Advent and the season of Epiphany. There is also November to consider. In most minds will also be the secular celebration of Christmas, which maps onto the liturgical calendar in the period from about October half term until probably Boxing Day. This secular celebration needs to be taken seriously. It was well described in *The Promise of his Glory* (PHG):

... there is the Christmas which begins with the tinsel-clad shopping days of mid-October. This 'winter season' is a relatively new arrival on the scene of the nation's commercial life, and for that reason Christmas has to live at times a double existence. It is solemnly celebrated on the correct day by devout congregations, and yet in practice celebrated in anticipation by millions of people, many on the fringe of religious observance, at Carol services and concerts, in schools and civic centres. Many people feel that Christmas is theirs, and not just the Church's, and this sense of ownership is true not only of Christmas: it is true of observances like those of Remembrance Sunday and the New Year, which have a vigorous and continuing existence as part of England's national life. (PHG, p. 2)

Almost 30 years have now passed since these words were written, and the 'winter season' is probably no longer a 'relatively new arrival', but the point was well made then and bears repeating now. The Church has an opportunity to engage the community in the wonderful story of the Incarnation, but it will almost certainly need to do so during November and December, not principally during the 12 days of Christmas. Although there is an almost instinctive irritation about this in the hearts and minds of liturgists like myself, that irritation probably needs to be moved past fairly swiftly by anyone engaged in public Christian ministry in order to embrace the opportunities of an extended Christmas season.

Those approaching this season in their own context are advised to undertake a complete ecclesiological and liturgical-theological analysis using the method outlined in Chapter 2, but a number of common threads will present themselves and we will explore these together here before moving on to a couple of worked examples.

Nesting seasons

Christmas

A glance at the Lectionary, or the contents page of *Common Worship: Times and Seasons*, reminds us we are dealing with a set of interlocking or 'nesting' seasons. As we noted above, the heart of this period is the Christmas season proper: formally in liturgical terms beginning on Christmas Eve at some point in the early evening with the First Evening Prayer of Christmas, which may very well in a number of places take the form of something more unstructured and informal such as a Crib Service, Christingle, or similar. This season ends at Epiphany, which is either celebrated on its proper day, 6 January, or on the Sunday between 2 and 8 January. Principal services during this Christmas season are likely to be the aforementioned Crib-type services, together with the ubiquitously popular Midnight Mass, and services on Christmas Day itself. The Canons remind us that Holy Communion must be celebrated on Christmas Day. In many places there may well be an additional and more informal 'all age' type Christmas morning service, or the principal service of Holy Communion might be appropriately shaped to appeal to a broad and potentially less-churched congregation. Due to school holidays, and the prevailing convention for post-Christmas time off, in many communities it might be quite difficult to sustain the Christmas celebrations even through the 12 days of Christmas. Later on in this chapter we will think a little about how to handle the Sundays and church buildings during this period immediately following Christmas.

Advent

Leading up to Christmas proper is the season of Advent, distinct and wonderful in the Christian tradition, but also effectively a four-week long anticipated Christmas for the wider community. Navigating this tension is difficult enough in any

Christian community that takes the liturgical year seriously, but the challenges are even more keenly felt by those organizing worship in a rural parish where, for example, demands for multiple carol services may well require worship with a strong Christmas theme to begin quite early on in Advent. CW: TS makes an attempt at recognizing this tension, but a certain liturgical stubbornness can be detected simply by the arrangement of material within the volume. Even given the expectation that in all but a very few communities Christmas carol services will need to be conducted prior to 25 December, all the resources for Christmas carol services are neatly filed within the Christmas, rather than Advent, section of the book and even more tellingly they come after the resources for Midnight Mass and the Christmas Day Eucharist! Now, I am a liturgist and I understand entirely why this arrangement was arrived at, but it does strike me as defending a border that for almost everyone was overrun a long time ago. Most clergy will therefore take the resources on CW: TS, pp. 88–91, and transpose them into the late Advent season. My instinct is that the Holy Spirit is considerably more elastic than most of us and if people are asking to come to church to celebrate Christmas on 20 December, they should only be welcomed.

That said, there is a wealth of material for the season of Advent itself and it is this Advent material which might lend itself to a parallel set of acts of worship that may not need to be tied as intimately to the specific geographical location as those for Christmas will be. For example, although a Christmas carol service and an act of worship on Christmas Eve and/or Christmas Day might well need to take place within the specific village worship building which has all those emotional and sociological ties to the people and the community, the same may not be true for the other imaginative provisions. CW: TS provides material for carol services of a distinctly Advent flavour, for example. Although this is likely to be something that will attract fewer people, perhaps it will allow a deeper and more theologically expounded interaction with themes of Advent: preparation, watchfulness and penitence. Perhaps there is potential here for something of an Advent carol service which might migrate around the churches of the parish year by year, or might be held in the building with the most appropriate liturgical setup for the liturgy in question. If something processional is envisaged, then we might choose the church with the greatest number of aisles. If something that might make use of imaginative lighting, audio-visuals and recorded music, then the church with the best electrical system is likely the winner. If there is to be fellowship as part of it, then seeking out the building with the most toilets, some running water and a decent heating system might be the priorities. We will return to Advent carol services later on and explore the potential options in CW.

The Sundays of Advent pose a challenge and an opportunity for rural communities. The prevailing tradition since the nineteenth-century importation from Europe of the Advent wreath is for this liturgical ceremony to be a central part of Sunday worship in the four Sundays leading up to Christmas. In both of my most recent rural contexts, however, the Sunday schedule in December, dominated by nativity services, additional afternoon or evening carol services and other interruptions to a regular schedule, means it is entirely possible there will not be an Advent act of worship on every Sunday in every church. We will explore some potential ways of reinterpreting the Advent wreath for the rural context, which might lend both the home and the school a more central place in our worship.

November

Although not part of Advent proper, and in the modern liturgical manuals firmly attached to the other end of the liturgical year, liturgical innovation in the Church of England since the early 1990s has led to the creation of a pseudo-season encapsulating the Sundays of November and wrapping up the Feast of All Saints, the Commemoration of All Souls, Remembrance Sunday and the Feast of Christ the King. This pseudo-season was introduced to the Church of England in 1991 in PHG, reflecting parallel liturgical work going on in the Society of St Francis and leading to the encouragement to consider a Season of the Kingdom (PHG, pp. 5–7). This season, frequently referred to colloquially even 30 years later as the 'Kingdom Season', actually never appeared in any official Church of England document under this title and currently exists under the rather clunky title of 'All Saints to Advent'. There are a number of potential real advantages to this season, as well as a couple of disadvantages. The advantages are that the themes of preparation, penitence and watchfulness which pervade the traditional Advent season are just as present in the readings and liturgical material for these four weeks of November. In communities where Advent gets overrun by Christmas early on, there is a real opportunity to explore the ideas of eschatology, the communion of the saints and even those classic advent themes the Four Last Things: death, judgement, heaven and hell. Kennedy notes that Advent has varied from four to at least six Sundays in length over the centuries as well as varying in tone from a period of severe penitence to joyful expectation (Kennedy, 2006, p. 5). With proper liturgical planning, a rural community can end up with almost eight weeks of Advent instead of just four, which could be a real blessing for a community keen to engage in these difficult but vital aspects of Christian doctrine.

The fundamental drawback with the innovation of a 'November season' (and indeed the same is true of the 'Epiphany season' created for *Common Worship* in 2000 but encouraged in PHG almost a decade earlier) is that effectively what is created is a dual calendar. The calendar of the BCP continues to number Sundays 'after Trinity' until the end of November. For rural parishes, many of which will have some churches within them which adhere more fixedly to the BCP calendar and liturgy, this can create a real mess in November where some churches are continuing to count the Sundays after Trinity, others are counting Sundays before Advent, the liturgical colour might well have changed in some churches, or for some services but not others, and the sense of disjunction can get quite uncomfortable. I remember writing service rotas in the Severnside Benefice which my poor churchwardens desperately tried to follow, which had entries in them like:

Remembrance Sunday (3 before Advent (Trinity 21))
(Red (Green at Chaceley))

On one level of course none of this really matters but it does work against the ambition of a sense of unity across a benefice. The introduction of the Feast of Christ the King, with the accompanying change of liturgical colour and distinctive themes, also somewhat displaces the traditional observation of 'Stir up Sunday', which again still has a particular appeal in some rural communities. The innovation around November and the Epiphany season are notable as rare occasions where the Church of England has made changes to a calendar which has maintained a fair degree of ecumenical agreement until the recent decades.

Remembrance Sunday procession in Tutshill

Epiphany

PHG, and then CW, made the developments to the calendar 'based on an evaluation of the season as a whole' (PHG, p. 6). The aim was to create (or recreate, by their argument) a unified season stretching from the beginning of November to the Feast of the Presentation of Christ in the Temple on 2 February. Thus, the Sundays and weeks after the Feast of the Epiphany on 6 January were 'beefed up' by renaming the Sundays as Sundays *of* rather than *after* Epiphany, reinforcing the Lectionary provision and suggesting staying in the white colour of Epiphany up until 2 February, rather than reverting to green as the Roman Catholic Church and many other provinces of the Anglican Communion do. What is created then is an extended season where the themes of light, revelation and proclamation are dominant, which creates space for some of the distinctive liturgies of Advent and Christmas to spill over into January. The Christmas crib remains a primary focus, together with the distinctive symbolism of the lighted candle. Services such as Christingle can find a place in this season. Candlemas becomes a confident end to an elongated season of Incarnation. In some places the Christmas tree remains displayed until 2 February. Some carefully selected Christmas carols might remain in the repertoire deep into January. Apart from anything else the psychological boost in the dark days of January is quite refreshing! The theological points being made are of course considerably deeper than that.

The drawbacks again are the feeling of discontinuity with the inherited tradition of the BCP, as well as, for some, a slight discomfort at having moved away from an ecumenically received calendar. The prevailing power of Twelfth Night in the consciousness of our nation is significant. Some will argue that the fact that some Christmas decorations and other evidence of festivity hang around in our buildings until the end of January creates an excellent opportunity for preaching and witness. Others might become slightly tired of having to explain to every baptism family or wedding couple that, 'no, we haven't just forgotten to take the decorations down!' Ministers and PCCs should simply note the permission given in CW to observe local custom and not feel too guilty if the end of this season becomes a bit ragged. I remember at least two years during my time at Severnside when I spent probably rather longer than was good for my spiritual life driving around the churches of the benefice in the middle of January reinstating white altar frontals and feeling slightly grumpy!

Potential areas for exploration

We have recognized that there is something important, ecclesiologically speaking, about the local at Christmas time in a rural community. We have identified therefore that there will be certain services, probably the Christmas carol service and the offering on Christmas Eve or Christmas Day, which are likely to need to be local. This presents a set of staffing and diary challenges which will vary depending on whether the rural benefice has three, seven or 15 buildings. We have also noted there are certain other opportunities during the Christmas cycle which might well not carry the same level of locality about their ecclesiology.

We have reviewed the broad provision for the Christmas Season, noting its highlights and also the distinctly elastic beginning and end of the season provided by November and Epiphany, respectively. We recognize the challenges this presents, particularly in communities where the BCP is a dominant liturgical form. We also recognize the potential opportunities for extending the season in imaginative ways.

What follows are a handful of outworkings of these principles to provoke exploration. Some of these are ideas I developed successfully in my own contexts and some were spectacularly *un*successful when I tried them, but might well work in other contexts! They are a discussion starter and an opportunity for reflection at the local level.

The local offerings

Christmas carol services

Liturgical purists might ideally see this service taking place somewhere in the true Christmas season, between the late afternoon of Christmas Eve and 5 January. Realistically, most of these Christmas carol services are likely to take place in the second half of Advent as evening services. We ought not pass over the possibility of carol services within the Christmas season, however. There are a number of imaginative possibilities, several of which lend themselves to the rural context particularly well. Chief among them is probably the potential for celebrating a festival of readings and carols on the Sunday after Christmas. The first Sunday to fall after Christmas Day has the tendency to feel like an anti-climax. If Christmas falls on a Saturday then the first Sunday of the Christmas season is Boxing Day where, with the best will in the world, attendance is likely to be low – except perhaps for churches dedicated to St Stephen! Conversely, if Christmas falls on a Monday or Tuesday, many people will have departed for their post-Christmas break by the time the first Sunday rolls around. Clergy may also be on holiday. A rationalization of the services offered on this Sunday in a multi-parochial benefice might well be appropriate and thought could be given to perhaps offering an early service of Holy Communion and then a Christmas carol service. Apart from the obvious benefit of not depending upon someone in priest's orders to conduct it, it has the much more theological virtue of maintaining the celebration of Christmas into the week following. The same order of service used for the Christmas carol services held in Advent could be used, or something slightly more informal could be concocted using one of the other sequences of readings provided in CW: TS. Particularly if the King's College, Cambridge sequence (sequence 3 in CW: TS, p. 91) is used before Christmas, one of the other sets of options might be selected in the post-Christmas days. Sequence 2 (CW: TS, pp. 90–91), which focuses on the Lucan Nativity narrative, has the virtue of pointing beyond Christmas to Candlemas which makes it particularly appropriate at the turning of the liturgical season. If a slightly less formal structure is desired then we might 'mine' the resources for Christingle and Crib services to create a Service of the Word, the skeleton of which is formed of readings and Christmas carols. If preaching was avoided in pre-Christmas carol services, this might also be an opportunity to preach. This service might be held in just one of the churches in the benefice, or perhaps repeated twice on the Sunday after Christmas: once in a mid-morning slot, and again in an early evening one. It is remarkable how much more willing people are to travel for a service after Christmas than before!

Modern Roman liturgical manuals remind us of the possibility of preceding Midnight Mass with a period of celebratory worship (see, for example, Elliott, p. 38). Although the Office of Readings is the liturgical model often suggested for this occasion, there would be no reason why a less Psalm-heavy offering might not be devised. If Midnight Mass is one of those services where the congregation gather very early, how about preceding the service itself with 45 minutes of 'carols around the crib', perhaps interspersed with some non-biblical readings? There are a number of easily accessible sources of devotional readings from the patristics, and poetry, some of which I list under the recommended reading.

Christmas carol services during the Advent weeks are much more likely, as we have said, to be local. The same outline order of service might be used repeatedly in successive churches, reducing the necessity for starting from scratch each time. An order of service with flexibility built into it will be able to adapt to the tone and musical resources of each individual parish church and also encompass a wider variety of ministries. While there may well be resistance to departing entirely from the nine lessons and carols formula, I have found that the introduction of one or two non-biblical readings tends to be popular and with a little thought some very pleasing liturgical connections can be made. One of my favourites is coupling some lines from the end of Charles Dickens' *A Christmas Carol* with the carol 'Joy to the World' so that the sequence runs directly from Scrooge proclaiming: 'It's Christmas Day! ... I haven't missed it!' into the congregation rising to sing, 'Joy to the world, the Lord has come! Let earth receive her King!' (Dickens, p. 88).

A real opportunity here is to connect things that might have happened earlier in Advent, perhaps in a school, nursing home or on a benefice scale, with the local acts of worship closer to

Christmas. When undertaking the liturgical-theological analysis of the Christmas season it is therefore worth flagging up the potential opportunities for symbols that have appeared earlier in the season. Would it be possible, for example, to use a large and impressive Advent wreath at the beginning of every local Christmas carol service? Perhaps lighting the candles and using a piece of liturgy such as that offered by CW: TS:

Today we remember Jesus and the story of his birth;
Jesus is our king.

As a candle is lit

Jesus Christ is the light of the world;
Jesus is our Way.

With Jesus even dark places are light;
Jesus is the Truth.

In Jesus we shall live forever:
Jesus is our Life. (CW: TS, p. 94)

At a service with many young children present, not only might children and their parents be selected to light, sequentially, the four candles on the wreath (assuming the service is taking place on or after the fourth Sunday of Advent!), but, using the permission given under Canon B5 to make non-substantive alterations to liturgical forms, we might simplify the liturgy above so every congregational response is identical. I have done this in a number of contexts so that very young children don't need to be able to read in order to participate. Replacing each of the congregational responses with the simple, 'Jesus is our King!' allows participation by non-literate members of the congregation and also allows liturgical responses to be used even when orders of service run out.

Another potential unifying element might be to construct the Crib during the carol service, so that if the crib figures have been making their way around the parish or benefice through Advent (see below) they can 'come home' to each local community as Christmas arrives.

Christmas Eve and Christmas Day

There are a number of 'in principle' decisions that affect what any rural parish offers over 24–25 December. Guiding factors will be a desire for some degree of parity across the communities, practical decisions around which churches can accommodate which type of services, how many leaders of public worship are available and of course how many buildings, parishes and villages we are talking about. I simply remind the reader of the ideal of beginning with the ecclesiology and the liturgical theology to ensure that our decision-making is Christ centred, rather than merely reactive.

In the Severnside benefice during my incumbency, we worked on the basis that given there were six buildings, roughly divided geographically into a western, central and eastern section of the benefice, the basic offering ought to be a midnight Eucharist and Christmas morning Eucharist in each of the three sections of the benefice. This would provide a principal service of Christmas in every church and community. It would also mean that for those who wished to attend church both at midnight and in the morning, both services would be accessible within a 10 minute or so drive. The times selected meant I could conduct one midnight mass and two of the morning services myself. The other services were led by retired or assistant clergy. During my tenure I rotated around the midnight services on a three-yearly cycle and between the two mid-morning Christmas Day services every other year. The benefits were a broad provision of worship which was pretty local. The drawback was I could not be present with all my people every Christmas. This was an example of an ecclesiology leading the decision-making: it mattered that worship was local on Christmas Day.

In the parish of Tidenham the decision-making leads to a slightly different outcome, partly due to a significant appetite for non-Eucharistic and fairly unstructured worship in the principal population centre of Tutshill. The same principles apply, however, with midnight services and Christmas Day Eucharists offered in both the north and south of the patch, with a non-Eucharistic offering at Tutshill, which attracts younger families. Like the Severnside benefice, this model requires two ordained priests, one in each of the two parishes. The all-age worship tends to be lay led, with the priest travelling from another church to Tutshill in time to conduct a quiet Holy Communion service after the all-age worship.

One of the bits of liturgical provision that has almost disappeared from the Church of England's usage, except in very 'high church' parishes, is the provision of the Vigil Mass of Christmas. Still very much part of the Roman Catholic tradition, this provides for a distinctive service of Holy Communion proper to the late afternoon or early evening of Christmas Eve. It is a fantastic option which is worth exploring, particularly in parishes where there might be a desire for a nocturnal celebration of Holy Communion but perhaps the congregation is unlikely to come out in great numbers in the middle of the night. Just to provide a little bit of background, the Church has traditionally supplied four different sets of readings and other proper material for services of Holy Communion celebrated at different times of the day on Christmas Day. They are the Vigil service, the service at midnight, the service at dawn and the service during the day. We can trace these sets of readings and other liturgical provision a long way back, certainly into the mediaeval Catholic usage. Three of those services survive into CW, where there are three sets of readings provided for Holy Communion on Christmas Day. Usefully, the Lectionary provides them chronologically even though it does not ascribe particular times of the day to them. Set I are the traditional readings for use at midnight, Set II are those traditionally used at dawn (perhaps appropriate for an 8 o'clock service) and Set III are the daytime readings. Interestingly the Vigil Mass as an entity did not re-emerge as an option when PHG and CW: TS emerged. The readings for the Vigil Mass have survived into CW, however, as the readings set for Evening Prayer on Christmas Day: Isaiah 62.1–5 and Matthew 1.18–25. Given that in very many communities Evening Prayer is unlikely to be said publicly on Christmas Day (the ministers having collapsed in a heap on a sofa by then!), it might well be worth considering rescuing these two readings from their relative oblivion and perhaps using them sometime between, say, 5 and 10pm on Christmas Eve for a celebration particularly aimed at the elderly, or indeed families with younger children who will struggle to come to church at midnight.

If one followed this type of modern Roman Catholic model, the service would be celebrated festally, in white or gold vestments, with Christmas carols and all the other celebratory aspects. Using these readings also restores Matthew's account of the Nativity to Christmas Day itself, which tends otherwise to be dominated by Luke and John.

The other service which is quite likely to occur sometime during the 24 hours of Christmas itself is some sort of all-age offering, as mentioned before, which might be called a Crib Service, a Christingle service, Carols around the Crib or an informal non-Eucharistic service on Christmas morning. In some communities more than one of these options will be undertaken. CW: TS provides quite a lot of material for this sort of service on pp. 92–104, which is well worth looking at. Alongside the official CW volume, it is well worth revisiting PHG as well as the Kennedy volume, both of which take rather more seriously than CW: TS the importance of non-Eucharistic worship and the connections between church, school and home. With some imagination, important links can be made with the worship offered in the local school and in peoples' homes over this period.

Not mentioned much, but something I have seen done really well in a rural context, is the adoption of the *Posada* tradition. The word itself is Spanish and translates as 'inn', or perhaps 'shelter', and there are a variety of ways in which this Latin American tradition can be imaginatively interpreted. At the heart of it is the idea that the crib figures of Mary and Joseph (and almost inevitably the donkey!) take a journey around the local community, depicting liturgically the journey of Mary and Joseph from Nazareth to Bethlehem. How this is done practically will be context dependent, but ideas might include the 'sending off' of Mary and Joseph, perhaps on the Feast of Christ the King, on Advent Sunday, or perhaps in the context of a school act of worship. The figures then spend the days of

Advent travelling around the community, spending the night in the homes of the congregation, perhaps also in the various schools, care homes, businesses or hostelries, until they end up coming back to church, probably at the service where the Crib is blessed. This could be the Christmas carol service, the Crib service, or indeed the Christmas morning service. The idea behind this tradition is to allow the liturgical worship to spill out into the community and where appropriate, and taking very great care to adhere to data protection and safeguarding legislation, photographs of Mary and Joseph staying the night in various places might be posted to an online Advent calendar, or on the parish website. This can be an excellent way of engaging a broad group of stakeholders if care is taken to be as inclusive as possible in terms of the overnight stopping points. In some contexts the *Posada* could take place around an entire team or united benefice. In other circumstances, the individual parish will be the proper context for the journey. In the parish of Tidenham, the *Posada* took place for many years, coordinated by the youth and children's ministry team but involving congregants of all ages and all the worshipping congregations within the parish. Everyone who had housed Mary and Joseph over December was then personally invited to join the rest of the congregation at a late afternoon service at Tutshill church where the crib was prepared and the climax of the liturgy was the placing of Mary and Joseph. The figure of the baby was placed the following morning during the main morning service.

Sacraments in stone: our buildings during Christmastide

We ought not to depart from this section on Christmas itself without thinking a little bit about how we use our buildings over the 12 days of Christmas. Where possible it is wonderful if the buildings can remain open during the period after Christmas when people might well be on holiday. Given the hours of daylight, we are probably only talking about buildings being open until about 4 o'clock in the afternoon, but given there is a natural instinct on the part of many people to 'get out and have a nice healthy walk' in the days after Christmas, coupled with the inevitable New Year's resolution to take more exercise, it is a real blessing if people encounter a church which is open. How about making sure that, if at all possible, the rota for locking and unlocking the church extends through the festive season and that, at least for the 12 days of Christmas, the treasurer can be persuaded to allow the heating to be left on? Where resources and copyright licensing allow, an extraordinarily wonderful atmosphere can be presented by having quiet festive music, or perhaps Taizé chants, playing during the course of the day. In the Severnside Benefice we selected one building, Apperley, on the basis of its place in the largest population centre, to host some simple but interactive Stations of the Nativity over a couple of Advent and Christmas periods. Simple foci for reflection and prayer are provided which can be used by individuals who happen to stumble upon them, as well as by visiting groups of schoolchildren, youth groups or adults. To offer just one example, the resources produced by Jumping Fish are excellent and are referenced in the recommended reading. With a bit of imagination local resources could also be devised. The key thing is for our buildings to speak the story as eloquently as possible, so any provision needs to be simple, clear, easy to set up and pack away (not least in the event of a post-Christmas funeral or wedding being scheduled) and the building needs to be obviously open (perhaps with a sign or poster to that effect), ideally warm, and beautifully decorated.

The prevailing message here is to resist the temptation to pack away Christmas on Boxing Day and allow the formal liturgical occasions to spill out into the wider community. If the daily offices continue to be said over the Christmas season, perhaps thought might be given to making these particularly accessible and inclusive, perhaps gathering around the Christmas Crib rather than in the usual place, and maybe changing the time to just before dusk in the case of Evening Prayer, to gather up any visitors?

Weaving a golden thread through the benefice

The Sundays of Advent

One of the most powerful ways to consider the Christmas season in terms of how to use symbols and teaching opportunities creatively is to spot where a 'golden thread' might weave its way through the lives of the people of the parishes. I believe familiar symbols such as the Christmas Crib, or indeed the Advent candles might offer a way of doing this. Objects of Christian devotion have endured because they work. While of course we need to safeguard against any erroneous idea that objects themselves are magical or powerful, nonetheless they speak to us deeply and among them the Advent wreath or crown, and the Christmas crib, are probably the most pervasive and powerful. In recent years, the Christingle has become similarly influential. CW: TS provides material for use with all three of these pieces of symbolism in church. What it fails to do, which is a great shame, is to follow PHG in providing a suite of material for worshipping with these symbols in the home. It is therefore well worth seeking out a copy of PHG and familiarizing ourselves with pp. 136–44 which provides:

For Church and Home

1 The Advent Wreath
2 The Jesse Tree
3 Table Prayers
4 Saturday Evening. (PHG, p. vi)

CW: TS deliberately omits this sort of material, pointing out there is a variety of material already published, but I regret the omission. What I think publishing this sort of material, designed for use in homes (and therefore by extension schools, care homes and potentially workplaces) alongside material primarily intended for use in churches, does is that a rather important piece of liturgical theology connects what happens in church with what happens in the rest of our lives. Making the point that we can carry our observations of Advent and Christmas out from the formal acts of worship into these other, nominally 'secular', environments is a really powerful piece of liturgical teaching which I strongly believe needs to be rediscovered. I commend the aforementioned section of PHG together with other material that holds before us the centrality of the home as an absolutely natural place for worship to occur. Kennedy provides some helpful background to all these principal Christmas symbols, noting particularly that the popularization of the use of Advent candles is taking up a practice which originated in an orphanage, which is well worth remembering (Kennedy, p. 66). Kennedy also points to another really useful volume of material designed for creating liturgical worship of a more elastic nature than CW: TS provides, in the excellent *Together for a Season*, also referenced in the recommended reading. The omission of resources for using a Jesse Tree in CW: TS is a real shame, and again Kennedy provides useful background and some practical and liturgical resources for a really creative act of worship (pp. 74–6).

Having noted above that in a rural multi-parish benefice it might be quite difficult to sustain the rhythm of the four Sundays of Advent with their distinctive themes and symbols, perhaps the Advent wreath itself might be a way of communicating those themes around the communities. If a sufficiently beautiful but portable Advent wreath could be either bought or, even better, constructed by a group within the parish, it could appear at a number of significant services and gatherings over the extended Christmas season, ideally including more secular events like the Christmas fayre, or Christmas lunches, where the overarching themes of Advent and Christmas could be subtly or more explicitly proclaimed simply by the presence of the wreath.

The most universal set of Advent themes recently is the sequence outlined in both PHG and CW: TS comprising the Patriarchs, the Prophets, John the Baptist and the Blessed Virgin Mary. These are by no means the only set of themes associated with Advent and in recent years the sequence whereby each candle symbolises sequentially hope, peace, joy and love has become increasingly popular. As recently as December 2020, Kramer noted that the development of the idea of Advent candles carrying themes is very recent, but that the practice has become so ubiquitous it is rare for them not to be simply taken as read. Indeed he cautions us against setting too much store by Advent themes, suggesting that by doing so we risk colluding with an Advent that is not much more than a countdown to Christmas. The article is well worth reading (Kramer, p. 31). Notwithstanding, themes are well-established and Kennedy provides an excellent summary of the biblical provision and associated themes for the Sundays of Advent (pp. 59–62). Note must be taken of the considerable difference between this sequence and that which the BCP provides. What is evident from Kennedy, as well as from the liturgical material in CW, is the deliberate attempt to provide a halfway point during Advent, where the tone shifts somewhat. The first half, from Advent Sunday to 16 December, gathers up themes of history, prophecy and eschatology and is probably closer to the Four Last Things (death, judgement, heaven and hell) as well as the predominant BCP themes for Advent. From 17 December, which will fall somewhere around the third Sunday of Advent, there is a shift to a focus on the biblical narratives leading up to the story of Christ's birth, centring around John the Baptist and Mary.

If it is not possible to sustain weekly thematic preaching and liturgical worship in every church in the benefice, the subtleties of the sequence will be lost. For a church that only has two Sunday morning services during Advent, for example, we might well end up lighting only the second and fourth Advent candle liturgically. A church which offers a mixture of CW and BCP lectionary provision will similarly experience a disjointed narrative. While there is no way of entirely resolving that, a parish that chooses to use one of the sets of Advent themes might find that a mixed economy of offering a substantial liturgical event for the whole benefice coupled, perhaps, with reinforcing the themes during weekly worship in the schools, care homes and other settings (ideally using the same Advent wreath that will be lit in church), may help to hold the themes prominently before parishioners' eyes, and also bridge the gap between the church building and the wider community.

While I am absolutely clear that this is not a book I have written merely to vent my own spleen about practices that irritate me, it might just be worth reflecting very briefly on the Advent candles themselves. Tradition seems to have arrived at candles which are either red or purple, although Kennedy reminds us that multicoloured candles were used in the original Advent wreath, and most of the liturgical manuals remind us that blue is also a traditional Advent colour. Any and all liturgical symbols are only valuable if they clarify, or enhance, theological truth about God. Conversely they become unhelpful, and indeed potentially idolatrous, if they make understanding God harder. I know I may be swimming against a mighty stream but I do wonder what the edifying nature of the pink or rose candle on an Advent wreath is when it is entirely divorced from its original purpose, which was to mirror the colour of the vestments and hangings of the third Sunday of Advent. I have sat in congregations and in liturgical training sessions where I have heard the reason for the pink candle being explained as symbolizing Mary, because pink is for a girl! I have also sat in congregations where the third purple candle is lit on Advent 3, and the pink one saved for Mary's Sunday, the week after! Given that most sets of Advent candles supply us with four purple candles and an optional rose coloured one, might it not be less confusing and misleading simply to use four purple candles if we are going to wear purple vestments throughout Advent? I actually rather like the use of rose vestments and the associated lightening of the Advent tone on Gaudete Sunday, but the candles are supposed to reflect the vestments and hangings, not the other way around, and I simply appeal for consistency and simplicity.

One really imaginative practice I came across was to invite worshippers to bring their own Advent wreaths to church either on the Feast of Christ the King, or the first Sunday of Advent, to be blessed. It might be much easier to manage a benefice service at the end of November than closer to Christmas, so perhaps this provides another option for dealing with Christ the King? Sadly, CW: TS doesn't provide any suggested prayers of blessing for either church or domestic Advent candles, but I offer the following as a potential framework:

> God of the patriarchs and the prophets,
> your son Jesus Christ is the Light of the World:
> as we hear the stories of your coming
> may these *[or + bless these]* candles which we have prepared
> *[that they may]*
> remind us of the promise of your glory,
> and make us ready to greet you when you come again;
> we ask it through the same Jesus Christ our King.

While in many rural churches the chances of having even one service on any given Sunday of Advent might be tricky, there is the question of how Advent candles are dealt with at an earlier service, if they are to be lit ceremonially at a mid-morning service, perhaps with the participation of young people. My solution to this, when it has arisen, is simply to buy more than one set of candles! That way the correct number of candles can be burning at an eight o'clock service, but then if required a brand-new candle can be deployed to be lit with ceremony later in the day. The relatively minor additional expense is well worth it to connect what is likely to be a smaller congregation with the ceremonies that are taking place at other times, and also tie such congregation in with some of the benefice-wide liturgies which might make use of the same candles.

Honouring the Advent themes

We reflected earlier on the possibility of making a real event of a principal and benefice-wide act of Advent worship, as an entirely separate and tonally distinct occasion to any Christmas carol service. Some slightly more rigorous liturgical-theological analysis is probably necessary when planning such a service. You might sit down with my analytical matrix and spend some time just thinking about Advent. There is such a plethora of resources available for this season that, as we discussed in Chapter 2, the danger of liturgical indigestion is real. A significant Advent offering for the entire benefice needs to take place in the most appropriate building for the event and knowing which the most appropriate building is will depend upon the results of your analysis and the theological truths that will be communicated. Alongside that there will be the challenge of gathering people at a dark and cold time of the year and there may need to be some convincing that an 'Advent carol service' is different enough from some of the things that will follow to be worth attending. Indeed, because of the potential for confusion it might be best to avoid using the title 'carol service' entirely, and opt for something like 'Music and Words for Advent', or shamelessly pillage something like 'From Darkness to Light' from Salisbury Cathedral.

What official provision is there? CW: TS provides some resources for carol services in the Advent Season, which offer some sets of themes. Three bidding prayers are suggested (pp. 44–5), all of which take subtly different approaches to Advent. These are well worth studying as part of the analysis of this season. All of them prefer the themes of justice, but with varying complementary tones of hope, judgement and repentance. Four sequences of readings are suggested (but not, of course, mandatory). The first culminates in one of the great judgement parables from Matthew, and is entitled 'The King and his kingdom'. The second sequence focuses on John the Baptist. The third culminates in the Parable of the Sheep and the Goats and has the imprisoned as a focus, picking up on the natural darkness of this time of the year. The final suggestion explores light, beginning with the Creation narrative and ending with words of Christ on his identity as Light of the world.

Alongside the suggestion of an Advent carol service and the Advent candles, CW: TS then suggests the other potential foci of the season might be the O Antiphons and the traditional text for the season, the Advent Prose, which begins, 'Pour down, you heavens, from above, and let the skies rain down righteousness.' Notable by their absence are any specific resources either for exploration of The Four Last Things, or the use of *Dies Irae*, the hymn 'Day of wrath and doom impending', which is another traditional text used at or just before the beginning of Advent and also associated with All Souls Day. PHG provides texts and suggested liturgical materials which make use of both these traditional liturgical forms, including a rather fine order of service for 'The Four Last Things: A Service of Preparation for the End', a non-Eucharistic act of worship with the twin themes of penitence and eschatology at the heart (PHG, pp. 102–11. For the *Dies Irae*, p. 121). Something really imaginative could be created with CW: TS, PHG and Kennedy open on the desk.

To use all this material would be to visit a liturgical stomach-ache upon your people. It might be that a cycle of themes could be adopted so the opportunity is taken to explore judgement, eschatology and issues of justice arising from the themes of darkness and light, in successive years.

Proclaiming the light into the New Year

The weeks of January provide an opportunity for an extended exploration of the Christmas themes of light, Incarnation and revelation. This is undoubtedly a harder sell in the local community, much of which will have packed up Christmas before New Year's Day. It does mean there is likely to be less pressure for very local liturgical celebrations and once the schools are back after Christmas there may well be an appetite for being involved in something jolly which will brighten up the end of January. The Christingle is the obvious candidate for such a service, either in school or in church. With careful selection of readings and carols, perhaps focusing on the journey of the Magi and the Candlemas story, something that confidently proclaims the victory of the light in the darkness could become a firm favourite of the January season.

Various suggestions for carol services in the Epiphany season and acts of worship focusing on the gifts of the Magi and the themes around Christian unity are provided in CW. With judicial use of these resources, together with some of the other sources we have already outlined, the shape of the season can be sketched out. A glance at the contents page for the Epiphany season (CW: TS, pp. 118–19) indicates there are three main staging posts in this season: the Epiphany itself, the Festival of the Baptism of Christ, and Candlemas. Alongside these three key points, two broader themes twine their way through the weeks of January: unity and mission. Neither are compulsory and once again it may be prudent to prioritize one theme at a time. The *Alternative Service Book* (ASB) had a series of themes around revelation in the post-Epiphany weeks and those themes are perhaps most explicit in the suggested order of service for the Day of Epiphany itself, with the miracles of Christ being expounded.

If we return to where we started: doing a proper analysis will lead us to a shape which is right for the season as a whole. My instinct is that, for most rural communities in the Church of England, this is likely to mean things being at their most local at the heart of the season with the potential for more benefice-wide 'one-off' specials increasing at each extreme of the season. Bearing in mind a pattern needs to be manageable and sustainable, this might mean launching the season with a distinctive Advent liturgy, concluding it with something similarly distinctive for the Epiphany–Candlemas season sometime in late January, or perhaps even on Candlemas Sunday itself, and keeping things local, duplicatable and intimate in the middle.

Crosses and candles on Candlemas Day: an example from Severnside

Depending on the date of Easter, the Presentation of Christ in the Temple can fall a month or so before the beginning of Lent, or very close indeed to Ash Wednesday. Either way, the themes of this distinctive and wonderful festival lend themselves to benefice-wide celebration.

In the Severnside Benefice I introduced a benefice service on the Sunday closest to Candlemas Day which had a distinct and radical shift of gear at the end of it, as the focus turned from the Crib to the Cross. Working on the basis that symbols are almost always more memorable than very long sermons, the liturgy progressed roughly as laid out in CW: TS until the post-communion prayer. After receiving communion, holding candles were distributed to the congregation while the ablutions were completed. At that point, the congregation sang selected verses of 'O come all ye faithful' during which there was a fairly informal procession from the Christmas Crib to the door of the church. What I tried to arrange to happen each year was that after everyone had received communion, but before the final hymn, the churchwardens brought out a large wooden Calvary Cross and set it up as quietly as possible next to the main door. Representatives from each parish were also invited to bring a cross from their own church (either a Calvary Cross, the cross from the altar, or from elsewhere). A lighted candle that had been burning before the crib was carried by a younger member of the congregation in procession to the door, and set in front of the large cross. The procession was arranged so the congregation would turn and, hopefully, be startled by the appearance of a symbol of Lent and Holy Week which had not been there when they arrived, just as we sang:

Child for us sinners, poor and in the manger,
fain we embrace thee with awe and love.
Who would not love thee, loving us so dearly?
O come let us adore him, Christ the Lord.

The carol ended with this verse, which makes explicit the relationship between the manger and the cross. One or more representatives from each parish then joined the group around the door, holding the crosses brought from their own church buildings. We then used the responses suggested in CW: TS (p. 204). Everyone blew out their candles at the suggested point in the responses:

Here we have greeted the light of the world.
Help us, who extinguish these candles,
never to forsake the light of Christ.

At the same time, the young person blew out the candle in front of the Calvary Cross. On occasions when I had persuaded the local congregation to keep the Christmas tree up and lit throughout Epiphany, the churchwarden also switched off the Christmas tree lights, which can be a rather dramatic symbol in a reasonably gloomy church! We then proceeded with the final three responses, at the end of which the representatives from each parish walked out in procession through the main door of the church, holding high the crosses which would be returned to their own buildings later that day.

Juxtaposition of Feast and Cross on Candlemas at Chaceley

The liturgical principles behind this kind of observation are clear, but it was also an opportunity to cement some benefice or team identity. Candlemas, forming the natural hinge between Christmas and Easter, is not predominantly a popular observance and so it made sense to take the opportunity to say some things about Christmas and Easter to the parishes as a whole. However, also using symbols which were regularly seen by the local congregation, such as the altar cross, it set up a connection which could then be preached on through Lent if desired.

It also had the practical benefit of providing a liturgical action which required at least one member of each congregation to be present, which automatically meant there would be representatives from all the churches. A procession appeals to almost everyone, but it took place entirely within the building and so was reasonably weatherproof!

Joining the threads

We have noted there is a strong and understandable impulse towards the local in the heart of the season, with the potential for doing things as a wider team or benefice probably being more likely to succeed in early December and late January. The questions are therefore around who is likely to participate in which events and how to make links across our geographical area where possible while honouring the distinctly incarnational message which has a locality about it.

Symbols are likely to speak louder than lots of words in this season. We have noted with regret the lack of provision in the authorized resources for making connections between church, school and home, but we have spotted where some of those resources may be found.

We have noted the importance of our buildings as sacraments in stone, particularly at this time of year, and advocated the use of the buildings, particularly during the 12 days of Christmas where there may be an increased footfall during the holiday period.

As we move on to think about the most significant and foundational of all the seasons of the Church's year, Holy Week and Easter, we will spot how very different this next season is, not only in terms of the narrative events of the scriptural account, but the distinctively different way in which the liturgies unfold. Our ecclesiological and liturgical analysis will be just as vital, but we are going to find it yields some significant differences as well.

4

Lent, Holy Week and Easter

Sharing Christ's own journey

The heart of what we will discuss in this chapter are the liturgies of Holy Week and, pre-eminent among them, the three days of the Easter Triduum. CW: TS reminds us:

> This *Pascha* ... was at first a night-long vigil, followed by the celebration of the Eucharist at cock-crow, and all the great themes of redemption were included within it: incarnation, suffering, death, resurrection, glorification. Over time, the *Pascha* developed into the articulated structure of Holy Week and Easter. Through participation in the whole sequence of services, the Christian shares in Christ's own journey. (CW: TS, p. 259)

While we are again dealing with a long season comprised of distinctive parts, this is something very different from the Advent and Christmas cycle. There is something significantly more linear about the Easter sequence and especially so for the very heart of it: Holy Week and Easter Day itself. As we analyse this season through our dual lenses of ecclesiology and liturgical theology, we are going to notice some family likeness in terms of the way in which we approach our ministry of teaching, worship and proclamation in a rural community. We are also going to notice some significant differences which have to do with the structure and configuration of the season as a whole, together with the fundamentally different way in which the secular world approaches Easter in our British context.

We will follow the same pattern as in the previous chapter:

glancing first through our two analytical lenses and then addressing the heart of the season and the length of the season, using some examples where appropriate.

A glance through the ecclesiological lens

Anyone who has ministered in a rural community will recognize the immediate differences in terms of the challenges of organizing the Easter observances as compared to those of Advent and Christmas. A good deal of the reason for these differences is ecclesiological. There is something different going on when we mark Lent, Holy Week and Easter and at least some of that has to do with the prevailing tone and emphasis of the season.

This book takes seriously the interconnected truths of the Incarnation and of redemption. At the beginning of Chapter 3, we noted that Christmas is a season which prefers the theological theme of Incarnation. We reflected on the way in which the truth of two parents and their baby sheltering in a borrowed stable speak powerfully to an attitude of locatedness and locality. Those themes are nothing like as evident in the Easter cycle. The prevailing tone here is that of redemption. Once again, I stress I am not attempting to separate incarnation from redemption in any way that would force a heresy in our doctrine of the atonement or in our Christology. It is true, however, that the part of the story which the Church's preaching and liturgical observance takes up here is the Way of the Cross. It is a following, with our Lord, through the events of his final few days on earth in Jerusalem and the surrounding area, through his betrayal, trial, conviction and execution, and then into the extraordinary silence of Holy Saturday and the joy of Easter morning.

At the heart of Christmas there is one simple story which we tend to tell several times and which engenders in the hearer, and in the local congregation, a sense of place and family. At Easter we are telling a very long story sequentially and no single part of it has that dominant strain of locatedness. Indeed the story, by degrees, disconnects us from our physical environment as we focus on a sequence of chapters in a story taking place in a very distinctive context. PHG refers to 'a series of ancient symbolic rites that originated in the Mediterranean' and which lend these observances a distinctive flavour (PHG, p. 2). This story then leads us to a distinct feeling of absence on Holy Saturday before a great celebration which is transcendental and mysterious in its tone.

This means we are faced with a different set of ecclesiological challenges when we consider Holy Week and Easter in the parishes. Though there are some occasions within the greater span of the season where there is a strong strain of locality and family, perhaps Mothering Sunday being pre-eminent, overall the challenge is not going to be managing the number of people who want to attend church during this season, but more likely working out how to tell the whole of this long and complicated story in local parish churches as well as the wider benefice. There is a huge amount of story to tell and once again capacity in a local ministry team is going to be an issue. This time it is not so much in responding to demand but in working out a sensible way in which to deliver a season that is almost 100 days long, from Ash Wednesday to Pentecost, and which has at its heart an intense few days of complicated liturgies. Some of the questions that will concern us are going to be about how we will manage this across multiple local communities. In how much of this story, realistically, will our people partake? How do we make sure the very heart of the story is told as clearly and powerfully as possible in our scattered rural community? Are there bits we can legitimately leave out? If so, which bits? And how does some of this connect to those other crucial parts of our community, like the school? Again, we are not dealing here with a secular season of celebration and it is much harder to anticipate Easter than it is to anticipate Christmas. Doing a Christmas carol service some 10 days before Christmas itself is almost automatic in most communities and people are well equipped to suspend their disbelief. The same is not so to anything like the same extent with Easter. Since the academic holidays have been actively decoupled from the religious observance of Easter in Britain, we are also faced with the fact that in some years the entire Spring term may be completed before the Easter Triduum begins, which makes telling the story in school considerably easier. In other years, with a very late Easter, schools may have broken up weeks before the arrival of Easter. This also has an effect on holidays and the presence or absence of our congregation, perhaps even of significant and key members of it. We may have to make our preparations for Holy Week and Easter with a number of our key folk away on holiday over the Easter period.

Another significant aspect of this season is the number of midweek observances. Whereas with Christmas, only the day itself is date-dependent and most of the most popular observances are translated to the nearest weekend, with this season we have Ash Wednesday, Maundy Thursday and Good Friday, all of which really don't work unless they are observed on the date. Ascension Day could be thrown into this mix as well, though there is increasing expectation (and tacit permission) to displace this to the following Sunday. With the former three, however, we are dealing with vital pieces of the story and with only Good Friday being a public holiday, we potentially have to face having a couple of significant parts of the story on a midweek evening when it is traditionally famously difficult to achieve a decent turnout in rural communities.

What is clear is that there are some significant ecclesiological considerations here and they are distinctly different from those of the preceding chapter. Imagination and some liturgical innovation will be required to allow the story of Easter to speak.

A glance through the liturgical-theological lens

There is a distinctly linear progression about this part of the liturgical year which is reliant to a great degree on telling different bits of the story sequentially and in the correct order. This is seen most clearly during the Triduum itself, where effectively the story begins on Maundy Thursday evening and just keeps going until Easter morning. Many liturgical commentators remind us we are effectively telling one story, and therefore the services are better thought of as one long service in and out of which we dip rather than discrete acts of worship. This is highlighted in the liturgical texts themselves by, for example, the absence of a blessing at the end of any act of worship once the Liturgy of Maundy Thursday begins. There is no blessing until the end of the first act of Easter worship, which reflects not only the sombre tone of the intervening liturgies but also the fact that we are effectively at one church service for the entirety of these three days.

The strength of the services of the Triduum is in this distinctive and extraordinary structure which carries us through the gamut of emotional, psychological, liturgical and theological content. From the relative praise and devotion of the early part of the Maundy Thursday liturgy, we move down the curve into the Garden of Gethsemane, further down into the stark austerity and abandonment of Good Friday and then, after the pause and accompanying emptiness and grief of Holy Saturday, suddenly up with a rush into the light of Easter morning. Those of us who are used to this journey, and who find in its heart-wrenching extremes perhaps the most perfect and wonderful revelation of the nature of God's love, want other people to experience this too. So rural clergy who are liturgically minded will want to offer this gift to their people. The question is, how? The strength of the Triduum is also its challenge for rural Christianity. It is necessarily sequential. We can't really anticipate much of it, and if we tried we would run the risk of evacuating the journey of its profundity. But we find ourselves in small communities, with many churches. There are some excellent modern liturgical manuals, which again you will find listed in the recommended reading, but almost all of them proceed from an expectation that, by and large, the same liturgical arena will be used for most of the principal liturgies during this season, and indeed that the same congregation will be present for all of them. So, for example, the space which is ceremonially stripped bare on Maundy Thursday evening is expected to be the same space into which the same worshippers enter again on Good Friday and again on Easter Day to be surprised and overjoyed by its transformation. Those of us who minister in multi-parochial benefices know that this expectation is almost certainly false. There may be some very fortunate rural parishes who can deliver the entire set of Holy Week and Easter services in every single church, duplicated across the benefice, and where a faithful and committed congregation will attend every one of the principal liturgies of the week, but that is not the norm. We have to make some decisions about venues and timings and we are reliant on proportionally much smaller congregations, different people living in different villages, and probably also having to interpret some of the liturgical manuals for a venue that does not have as much kit, or people, or basic resources like decent heating or running water as are taken for granted by these books which tend to assume a suburban or urban context. Nevertheless there are some imaginative ways to help the Easter story sing in this sort of context, and that is what we will explore here.

Linear seasons

The Easter Triduum

Just as Christmas Day and its 12-day season is the heart of the Christmas cycle, so the Great Three Days, the Holy Triduum which runs from the evening of Maundy Thursday to the celebration of the Resurrection on Easter morning, is the absolute heart of the Easter cycle. Its provenance is ancient and texts such as those of Gordon-Taylor and Jones, or of Bradshaw, both listed in the recommended reading, provide the student with a good starting point for revising the history of these observances. The first significant difference we note is we are dealing with three days, rather than one day, at the heart of what we are about. The sacred ceremonies and rites of the Church which we receive in the tradition, and which have been revived and refreshed in CW: TS, following the innovations of the earlier volume, *Lent, Holy Week and Easter* (LHWE), contain the treasuries of our marking of the culmination of our Lord's earthly life.

At the heart of what is happening is a journey, a journey of remembrance. Just as at every Eucharist we remember, in the proper sense of that word, so in this extended act of liturgical worship over three days we enter into this complex process of remembering, imagining, participating and reflecting upon the final hours of Jesus' earthly life.

Maundy Thursday, properly, begins in the evening of the Thursday of Holy Week. Very occasionally in traditional liturgical documents you might find the services of the morning and afternoon of this day listed as services of 'Holy Thursday', though the practice of referring to the entire 24-hour period as Maundy Thursday is now almost universal. We have clues, however, in our lectionaries and liturgical books. You will notice the Collect of Maundy Thursday and the colour white are set only for the evening Eucharist. The expectation is that, for any other services that day, perhaps morning and evening prayer, the liturgical colour remains as it was on the previous three days and the Collect for Palm Sunday is used. The point is there is a radical shift in the *evening* of the Thursday of Holy Week. This is where we enter into the most ancient part of the liturgy. From the beginning of the Liturgy of Maundy Thursday we are effectively beginning one long service which will last until our first celebration of Easter, either late at night on Holy Saturday, or early in the morning on Easter Day. The tone changes at that late afternoon or early evening point where we begin the service in which the Last Supper is recalled, perhaps feet are washed, the institution of Holy Communion is celebrated, and then the darkness gathers as we move to Gethsemane and look towards Good Friday. Holding the Triduum together is probably the principal task for the rural liturgical leader. I will offer some imaginative possibilities below which may be able to be mapped perfectly onto your context, but will more than likely simply be conversation starters. The ecclesiological and theological point is this however: in these three days we remember the most fundamentally important, transformative and salvific events of the Christian faith and these three days therefore are a gift to the Church which we, in our rural communities, need to cherish, hand on and interpret for our context.

So Maundy Thursday evening begins this Triduum. Good Friday is next, with its distinctive focus on the Cross. CW: TS provides a set of resources for a principal act of worship on Good Friday, with or without the celebration of Holy Communion. Resources like the Kennedy with Haselock volume, or *Together for a Season*, provide additional and complementary imaginative material. LHWE is also well worth picking up again. Like PHG, some of the more creative material didn't make it into the CW provision, but it is still useful and worthy of consideration. The heart of the service of Good Friday is a reflection upon the cross and in some places this will likely be something a bit more like the 'Three Hours' para-liturgical service of hymns, sermons and silence. Other places will want to go for something that looks more like the Liturgy of Good Friday with its fourfold shape: Gathering, Word, Prayers and Devotions at the Cross, with an optional receiving of Holy Communion. In many places, something oriented specifically towards younger children may also be a priority. Marking the distinctiveness of this day to those who might only attend on Good Friday and trying not to anticipate Easter while communicating the entirety of the story, particularly the strains of hope, is a perennial challenge.

Holy Saturday struggles to maintain its identity for a number of reasons, not least the fact that it has at least three names! *Common Worship* tends to opt for Easter Eve, which personally I find a less helpful title than Holy Saturday. The former has a bit too much of the fizz and excitement of Christmas Eve about it, which doesn't help our teaching about the emptiness of the day. The rest of the world will be calling this day Easter Saturday, which of course liturgically speaking is still seven days away! Either way, the prevailing liturgical message of this day is emptiness. This is a valuable and integral part of the Triduum because it is the day on which 'God is dead'. It is the opportunity for reflecting on the emptiness and anguish of grief, and has great potential if the liturgy of this day is done well. In fact, there is no distinctive liturgy for Holy Saturday, explicitly because you don't really do anything when God is dead except grieve. The heavily abbreviated orders for morning and evening prayer are all that is required, perhaps together with some devotional material, poetry or readings from the Church Fathers. Holy Saturday can be an extraordinarily powerful experience if done well.

The practical challenge, perhaps particularly for beautiful and popular rural churches, is that many people will want to get married on this day. This is a significant pastoral dilemma. All I would say is, for churches who want to take the Triduum seriously, it behoves them to communicate clearly, compassionately and perhaps most importantly, a long time in advance, if there are any days on which weddings may not be solemnized in that parish or benefice. It was my practice in the Severnside Benefice not to book weddings during the Triduum and this was made clear on the booking schedule at least 24 months in advance. When I first arrived in the parish I inherited a wedding on Holy Saturday, which of course I conducted. This is a specific example of the way in which liturgical planning works best if it is based on a confident theology and ecclesiology, communicated clearly across the parishes and, vitally, explained a long way in advance to those who might seek the ministry of the church during these days. One of my offers to a couple hoping to be married on Holy Saturday was to suggest that I would love to conduct their wedding on Easter Day, or Easter Monday. This was an offer which was taken up more than once.

The other potentially complicated conversation that might occur over Holy Saturday is with those who arrange the flowers! Here, again, there needs to be compromise. My ideal compromise, which I found to be workable, was that flower arranging would not begin until mid-morning at the earliest on Holy Saturday and where possible morning prayer would be said publicly in the stripped and empty space before any evidence of flower arranging paraphernalia were introduced. In addition, I implored my churchwardens not to dress the altars et cetera in the festal hangings until late afternoon, which at least held the starkness of the day before visitors and flower arrangers alike. It might be possible to say evening prayer quite early on Holy Saturday, perhaps at three or four o'clock, and only after this has been completed, put the white hangings on the altar, pulpit and lectern. I have encountered churches where freshly arranged flowers were veiled in very lightweight black material once arranged, which might be a potential option if your church building is likely to receive visitors during the day or if public evening prayer will be offered.

The Great Day of Days is, of course, Easter. This celebration might begin after dark on Holy Saturday evening or might happen before or at dawn on Easter Day. Even if none of these options is taken up, it is likely to include an early celebration of Holy Communion and one or more services in the mid-morning.

Holy Week and Easter Week

The Triduum nests within an extended fortnight, beginning on Palm Sunday and ending on what CW describes as the Second Sunday of Easter (the First Sunday after Easter according to BCP) and to which many of us still habitually refer as Low Sunday. This fortnight gives the Triduum room to breathe, as it were, and also makes a number of important theological points. Palm Sunday begins the fortnight and again has two distinctive liturgical elements: the procession and the proclamation of the Passion Gospel. Some communities will do both of these elements every year, others might prioritize one over the other. We will discuss some potential ways of doing this. Palm Sunday evening is an underused resource. It provides an opportunity for a liturgy that tells the story of the coming week in a bit more detail, and probably with more preaching, than is possible in the morning. It has become unfashionable to preach at the Palm Sunday liturgy though in fact CW: TS expects a sermon, as did LHWE, and I strongly recommend preaching, albeit briefly. I fear the standard comment that 'the gospel can preach itself today' overestimates the Christian literacy of even some of our most faithful churchgoers. It may also indicate an instinctive nervousness on our own part when it comes to preaching about the Atonement.

The first three days of Holy Week (and indeed the morning and afternoon of Thursday) have a distinctive tone. The readings set for morning and evening prayer, and for the daily Eucharist, begin to carry us into deep waters of biblical reflection on atonement, salvation, sinfulness and judgement. Wherever it is possible to particularly advertise daily services during this period this should be done, but care needs to be taken not to provide opportunity for people to worship early in the week in a way that might lead them to opt out of something later in the week. The weekdays of Holy Week are not a priority if the payoff is a lower attendance during the Triduum. There might be imaginative things to be done with the building, in a similar way to those suggested for Christmas.

Easter Week is very much like the 12 days of Christmas: wonderful, full of potential, and almost everybody is asleep or on holiday! Much of what I have said in the previous chapter applies here too. The strain of praise and celebration needs to be carried on for as long as possible into Eastertide, and the Sunday after Easter Day could be an opportunity for something that mirrors the post-Christmas carol service: a benefice service of Easter praise perhaps? In some years, a number of the calendar dates of red-letter feast days might fall in Easter week as well. The rules tell us we are not allowed to celebrate such feasts in Holy or Easter Week but rather transfer them into the week following Low Sunday. It is not uncommon for the Feasts of Mark and George to fall during this period, and indeed in some years for the Annunciation to be similarly transferred. Most of the time only fairly regular churchgoers will notice Annunciation or Mark, but when St George's Day falls during this fortnight and has to be transferred that can cause confusion and problems particularly if there is a tradition of a more secular observance of England's patron saint in your patch.

Lent

We noted earlier this whole season is something like a hundred days long. It begins in February or March with Ash Wednesday and the period of Lent leads us up to Holy Week. Like Advent, there are a number of challenges for rural benefices around telling the story of Lent consistently on what is likely to be a four-week service schedule. Unlike Advent, Lent is unlikely to be crowded out by 'popular' observances, except perhaps for a pre-Easter school service in years when the term ends a long time before Easter. Depending on your policy on weddings during Lent, there may also be a relative lack of pastoral offices and therefore it might be possible to hold the six weeks of Lent as a bit of a retreat for the entire benefice. For several years I successfully managed to move all non-essential meetings out of Lent and used the space for a programme of home groups, *lectio divina* groups and enhanced presence in the schools. It was a way of inviting the entire benefice into praying Lent in a slightly different way. It worked better in years when Easter was early, and therefore the APCMs fell in Eastertide!

Ash Wednesday is the obvious occasion for something ben-efice-wide and might draw a reasonable congregation if it is celebrated in only one church. The weather and the date of Easter will invariably have an effect on this but it is worth persevering with. The sermon on this day can lay out the jour-ney that lies ahead and fill in some of the gaps where there might be inconsistent preaching over the coming weeks. It is entirely possible to take an Ash Wednesday service in school, including the imposition of ashes and where I have done this it has been profoundly moving. The liturgy needs to be pre-pared carefully with special regard for appropriate parental permissions and safeguarding needs to be taken, as always, very seriously. It is entirely possible, and indeed traditional, for ashes to be imposed outside of the Eucharist where nec-essary or appropriate. CW: TS does not offer this possibility, which is a shame. It is also possible, and indeed encouraged by Elliott in the Roman Catholic context, to retain some of the Ashes and distribute them, using an appropriate form, to those who were genuinely unable to attend on Ash Wednesday (see Elliott, pp. 55–7). He identifies the housebound in particular, and offering ashing as well as Holy Communion to those worshippers who are confined to their homes, or care homes, during Lent can be a particularly powerful and well received ministry. I have also, from time to time, offered the imposition of ashes after church on the First Sunday of Lent for those who could not attend on Ash Wednesday. I have tended not to advertise this in advance for fear that people will stay away on Ash Wednesday, knowing that ashes would be available on the Sunday. This is undoubtedly tricky terrain to negotiate!

A tradition well worth rediscovering is that of 'burying the Alleluia' either on the Sunday next before Lent or on Shrove Tuesday. More frequently observed in the USA, this rather lovely tradition involves having a board, scroll or paper with the word 'Alleluia' prominently inscribed. This is either physically buried in the churchyard, perhaps close to where the Easter Garden will appear, or symbolically hidden under an altar, to be 'discovered' again on Easter Day. This provides an excellent teaching moment for children and young people in school or church about the absence of the word 'alleluia' during the forthcoming season.

Probably the most 'popular' service during Lent is that of Mothering Sunday. Its position in the middle of Lent creates both challenges and opportunities. This is probably the Sunday on which most churches will want their own local service, which could have implications for the service schedule and the teaching during Lent. There is also an expectation in some places that baptism might be administered on Mothering Sunday, even if it is strongly discouraged during the rest of Lent. The tradition, particularly in Britain, of this largely secular celebration undoubtedly provides great opportunities for our churches and needs to be embraced while maintaining in some measure the tone of the season. Care must also be taken to avoid unwittingly falling into the trap of celebrating the structure and make up of one particular type of family to the exclusion of others, or stirring up deep emotions in the bereaved without the appropriate pastoral support being present. CW does its best to maintain something of the tone of Lent in the provision of the readings for Mothering Sunday and with appropriate selection, perhaps particularly of the Exodus reading alongside the narrative of Mary at the foot of the cross, the themes can be complementary rather than jarring. Where possible, the readings for the Principal Service of the Fourth Sunday of Lent should be used somewhere else on the day.

The last full week of Lent prior to Holy Week is designated as 'Passiontide', though this rather esoteric title appearing in the Lectionary can cause as much confusion as anything else. The idea is that for this fifth full week of Lent, something of the tone of Holy Week can be anticipated. CW: TS provides a set of distinctive liturgical elements for this week. In some traditions, notably those that follow the 'Use of Sarum', there might be a change of liturgical colour on the Fifth Sunday of Lent from the unbleached linen 'Lent array' of the early part of the season to the red of Passiontide. This is undoubtedly powerful where it is used, but is not widespread. Certainly there is the opportunity for hymns and songs to be introduced from the Fifth Sunday of Lent which have the cross as their focus. The Fifth Sunday of Lent is sometimes referred to as Passion Sunday and provides another opportunity for a whole benefice act of worship, where the theme and tone can anticipate the journey of Holy Week.

Eastertide

Modern liturgical revision has firmly established an Eastertide of 50, rather than 40, days. By this reckoning, Easter ends after the final act of worship on the day of Pentecost. The use of 'alleluia' in the hymnody and liturgy continues with abandon until Pentecost, and we are encouraged to continue to use Easter hymns and songs to some degree throughout the season. The staging post in this season, rather in the way that Passiontide marks a change in tone during Lent, is the celebration of the Ascension. Properly kept on the fortieth day after Easter, always therefore a Thursday, this Feast day ushers in nine days of preparation for celebrating the coming of the Holy Spirit on the day of Pentecost. While there is no formal permission granted at present to translate Ascension Day to the nearest Sunday (unlike the permission given to do so with Epiphany, Candlemas and All Saints Day, or indeed the permission given in many parts of the Roman Catholic Church), many will instinctively want to do much of the Ascension teaching on the Seventh Sunday of Easter. The Lectionary doesn't preclude this, but certainly makes the task harder by favouring themes of the coming of the Holy Spirit. Where possible, keeping Ascension on its proper day holds the integrity of the 40 days of the biblical account. Also, falling in the late spring, there are possibilities for open-air worship or early-morning worship, which might make a midweek gathering more appealing. In the Parish of Tidenham there is a parish breakfast served after a 6am Eucharist, which is surprisingly popular. It may well be that the principal draw is the excellent breakfast, but no matter! I have experimented with services at midday (which psychologically feels right to me) and in the evening. Neither have drawn huge crowds, but I believe they are well worth persevering with. I rather regret there is no encouragement to change the liturgical colour for the last nine days to the red of Pentecost. I understand the liturgical rationale: the prevailing season is still Easter, and the splash of red on the day itself is certainly joyful and powerful. Local tradition might choose to anticipate Pentecost in colour to accompany the distinctly Spirit-oriented readings. Earlier liturgical tradition associated the burning paschal candle rather more with the physical presence of Jesus on earth after his resurrection and led to a ceremonial extinguishing of the paschal candle after the gospel reading on Ascension Day. We are now encouraged to consider the paschal candle to be much more a symbol of the enduring presence of Jesus with his people until the end of times. So, although there is a brief optional liturgy provided in CW: TS (p. 501) for the ceremonial extinguishing of the paschal candle on the day of Pentecost, I actually think this confuses the symbolism rather than enhancing it. I would commend, the day after Pentecost, the practice of simply moving the paschal candle privately to a position close to the font, where it remains for the rest of the year.

Our brief recap of this season shows how long it is and quite how many shifts and changes of emphasis and tone there are. This makes it the more important to begin planning early and ideally to do at least some of that planning through the ecclesiological and liturgical lenses this book advocates. What are the key moments? Where are the key places at various times? As at Christmas, there are distinctly local moments but much more opportunity for doing things creatively across the benefice or team as well. Partly this has to do with the likelihood of better weather and more daylight, but it also has to do with the nature of this season as, above all, the telling of a wonderful and exciting story which keeps unfolding as we go.

The local offerings

If we proceed on the basis that there are certain moments when each church is likely to have a strong desire for its own local act of worship, and that there are the moments where this is not such a priority, I suspect Mothering Day and Easter Day are likely to be the key moments where a local act of worship is most important during this season. These, therefore, are probably the moments in the service schedule to programme in an expectation for a local act of worship. These expectations need not necessarily include a service of Holy Communion because those can continue to be distributed around the benefice or team, but it is likely to be very important for the lights to be on and for something liturgical to be happening.

Sacraments in stone: our buildings during Easter?

As you undertake the ecclesiological and liturgical-theological analysis of your own benefice, one of the things that might spring to mind is what we might do with our buildings which are open, but not necessarily being used on any given day. For

example, let's take Good Friday. Imagine you are going to distribute your principal Holy Week services around the benefice
and one or more of your churches are going to host neither a
Maundy Thursday evening, nor a Good Friday service. What
might you do with that building over the couple of days which
are so dramatic and powerful in terms of telling the story of
our salvation, but in which neither of those pieces of the story
will actually be told liturgically?

We have been building up a narrative of the impact of rural
church buildings, and indeed their churchyards, which reminds
us how important they are to their communities. One of the
reasons they are so important is that they are very often open
and are used in an ad hoc manner. It must surely be the ideal
that anyone who stumbles into our buildings on Good Friday
will be able to soak up something of the power of this day in
the Church's year even if nothing liturgical is happening. The
question, in this instance, is whether we strip every one of our
church buildings bare on Maundy Thursday evening, and then
redress them sometime on Saturday, even if nothing liturgical
happens in those intervening hours. I think if we can, we should
try to tell the story of salvation visually. It is interesting that the
modern Roman Catholic liturgical manuals take a very different
stance. Elliott, for example, encourages the Maundy Thursday
liturgy to take place with a gathered congregation from a
number of different churches, which is exactly what I am about
to argue below. He then, however, goes on to make an argument which is one of the reasons I have written this book in the
first place. Talking about the Maundy Thursday service, with
the reservation of the Blessed Sacrament at the altar of repose,
and the associated stripping of the sanctuary, he notes, 'the
Transfer of the Eucharist is only carried out in churches where
the Good Friday afternoon liturgy will be celebrated' (Elliott,
p. 104). Interpreting the Roman Catholic liturgical directions
for parishes of an Anglo-Catholic temperament in the Church
of England, the annual *Order for the Eucharist* similarly notes,
'if there will be no Good Friday Liturgy in the same church,
the Blessed Sacrament is replaced in the Tabernacle and Mass
ends in the ordinary way' (Hunwicke, p. 23). What Elliott and

Hunwicke argue is probably sound if we take a very literal approach to the sequence of Holy Week liturgies, but it misses the point that the building itself is a sacrament and never more so than when it is at the heart of rural community. I would argue that, if possible, allowing our buildings to speak the story of Holy Week and Easter, even if there is no gathered liturgical event happening in that particular building on one of the main days of the week, is not only a good thing to do, but actually is doing something importantly incarnational in the context of rural community. Is it possible, then, for every church in the parish or benefice to be stripped bare for Good Friday? Or indeed to have palm crosses available in them over the preceding weekend, even if there will not be a Palm Sunday service? Might there, at least, be some personalized prayer cards available so visitors stumbling into the church on Good Friday, surprised by the stark and empty atmosphere, are invited to ponder on the reason for that, and also perhaps invited to come back on Sunday to witness the transformation? Might we use our churchyards similarly? Where our churchyard still has a preaching cross it could be appropriately adorned, or otherwise a large wooden cross could be set up for the period between Passion Sunday and Pentecost, sequentially adorned with palm fronds, a purple or scarlet hanging which is replaced with a white one, or a mass of flowers, on Easter day. The coronavirus lockdown of 2020 saw a significant amount of innovation in this area as congregations came to terms with their churchyards being the only permitted arenas for visual symbols of the season.

Jumping Fish publications have a series of simple stational resources, and their offering for this season is called *Experience Easter*. They also have a version of this resource called *Experience Easter Outside* which lends itself to a school playground, or to the churchyard. If there will be very few services in church over Holy Week, what about setting up the church as an interactive worship space for the week? Indeed, if it were done early enough, perhaps the local school could be invited to come by classes to walk the stations together? As with the advice I offered in Advent, some appropriate Lenten music playing quietly in the background would enhance the atmosphere of prayer.

While it is always important to consider and explore the relationship between public liturgy and opportunities for private prayer, it is particularly so in our rural communities where the church and the churchyard are often held in high regard by those who may rarely come to an act of public liturgy.

Proclaiming salvation through the benefice

We have already rehearsed the particular practical challenges facing rural ministers at festival seasons: many buildings, several schools, relatively few people, relatively little disposable capital, probably fewer bits of liturgical paraphernalia, the challenge of worshipper fatigue and questions of duplication of services. I have suggested that the two days on which it is likely an act of worship in each individual church is most appreciated and valuable, if a prioritization has to be made, are Mothering Sunday and Easter Day. It is equally possible that in some communities a simple daily act of morning and/or evening prayer is sustainable, particularly if it is lay led.

What is less likely to be either appealing or advisable in many multi-parochial benefices is attempting to deliver the entire week of Holy Week services in every single church. Partly this is simply to do with resources. Partly it is also to do with the ecclesiological difference between the Christmas season and the Easter one. The story of Holy Week is about the discovery of the breadth, depth, height and width of God's love. It is probably best journeyed together, if possible, and so I advocate an early exploration of the analytical matrix that I describe in Chapter 2, which might give you, as local ministers, a clearer idea of what the key moments in this journey are and where, in your particular context, these liturgical episodes might take place. Vitally, also, you might discover ways of connecting the distinct liturgies in a way that not only tells the story of God's love but also helps to build and retell the story of the local community. I will describe a couple of examples from the Severnside Benefice in a moment.

The whole journey

Paramount to a successful liturgical observation of Holy Week in a multi-parochial benefice is getting the shape and development of the journey straight in our heads early on. What is the journey on which we wish to take our people? How will those who choose to participate in it experience the journey? How will it strengthen and inform their faith? And, perhaps particularly important for rural communities, how will each part of the journey strengthen and inform the faith of those who choose to turn up only to the event happening in their local church? How can we make sure that each nugget speaks of salvation even when decoupled from the whole? Your answer will be different from mine but there will be common threads.

Because of the number of churches I had in Severnside, and because we had something of a tradition of meeting together on fifth Sundays, my instinct was to try to do the principal moments of the Easter journey together but then to keep returning to each local church regularly. My pattern was therefore going to look something like regular Sunday services on almost all the Sundays of Lent and Eastertide, but with benefice services on the 'flagship' days of the journey. My decision was to try to hold the entire liturgical cycle as one, and so I planned for the entire journey from Ash Wednesday to Pentecost. This worked well for me because of the number of churches I had and because although the benefice was big, it was only ever actually a 20 minute or so drive from any one of the villages to the furthest flung church. For a much larger benefice or team, your decision might be to try to do Holy Week together, but to deal with the periods of Lent and Easter separately.

My schema identified Ash Wednesday, Palm Sunday, Maundy Thursday, Good Friday, the Easter Vigil and Ascension Day as my six moments where I would encourage the entire benefice to come together. These would be the 'hooks' on which I would hang my systematic preaching of the season. For that reason I would preach at all of these services, at least in the first year. There's something about consistency of vision which might help to hang the observances together. Having identified these six principal liturgies, I then needed to make a decision, with my team, about the venues. Some of those decisions were practical: Ash Wednesday and Maundy Thursday would be happening in the dark so a church with reasonable parking and external lighting would help. Maundy Thursday needs space for foot washing so a church with slightly more flexible seating would help. The Easter Vigil is the most complicated of the liturgies needing, among other things, a fire, a decent font and so on.

In the illustrations that will follow, we decided the distribution of the liturgies that would work best for us were as follows (see Figure 2 on page xxix to orient yourself):

Ash Wednesday: St John the Baptist, Tredington, which has a large chancel to allow us to sit in a semicircle around the altar for the ashing and for the Eucharist.

Palm Sunday: The Methodist Chapel and Holy Trinity, Apperley, because these two churches are less than 15 minutes' walk from each other, therefore allowing not only an opportunity for a genuine ecumenical act of worship but also a procession from one liturgical space to another, rather than just a walk around the inside or outside of a single church. On other years it would also be possible to do the same thing in villages which possessed a village hall or, in the case of Deerhurst, seeking permission from English Heritage to use Odda's Chapel.

Maundy Thursday: St Mary, Deerhurst, principally because the two key liturgical symbols I wanted to draw out were the foot washing and the stripping of the altar. St Mary Deerhurst has a 'Reformation style' chancel with seating all around the altar, therefore allowing the entire service to take place in the round, lending itself perfectly to drawing out the symbols of community being gathered and then scattered. I often feel the stripping of the altar can feel a little remote from the congregation if they are a very long way away, but in this instance everyone could see clearly this profound liturgical action.

Seating in the round at Deerhurst Church

Good Friday: St Mary, Forthampton, or St John the Baptist, Chaceley, chosen principally because they are both a comfortable two or three hours walk from Deerhurst, which was vital for my plan for uniting the liturgies of Maundy Thursday and Good Friday (see below). Both of them also have the benefit of being quite formal liturgical spaces. Gordon-Taylor and Jones note, and I agree with them, that changes in the liturgical arrangement of worship spaces over Holy Week can enhance the storytelling (p. 44). While Maundy Thursday lends itself to an intimate 'in the round' setting, Good Friday, with its stark liturgical austerity, works best in a formal east-facing environment. For this reason Forthampton and Chaceley, with fixed pews and large altars up against the east wall of the sanctuary, were perfect and struck an ideal contrast.

The Easter Vigil: Tewkesbury Abbey. Here is a moment where I decided that, actually, while I was perfectly capable of delivering the liturgy myself, and a good deal of me wanted to do so, the complexity and beauty of the Vigil would best be experienced in a larger worship centre. We were lucky to be very close to the town of Tewkesbury with its splendid and liturgically renowned Abbey Church. By negotiation we all attended the liturgy there, some of our number participating liturgically as servers or clergy sitting in choir. One cleric, often but not always me, took the principal paschal candle from the benefice to be lit from the Abbey's candle at a given point in the liturgy and then carried back to the benefice. I encourage you to consider whether this might be something that would work in your context, particularly if you have a good relationship with a larger minster or cathedral church in your vicinity. I have heard of deaneries coming together to participate in a joint Vigil service as well.

Ascension Day, St James the Great, Stoke Orchard. Because this church is on one of the furthest extremes of the benefice, and the smallest of the six churches, it lent itself best to a late spring/early summer liturgy. It is set in a gorgeous churchyard with a view out through the clear east window into a graveyard buzzing with bees and waving spring flowers. By the time this liturgy came around it would be light in the evenings, warmer, and therefore conducive to an act of worship in this environment.

Your decision-making may lead you to entirely different local conclusions when you plan the span of worship from mid-February to June, but the key thing is to make those decisions with both ecclesiological and liturgical-theological lenses operative.

Holy Week

Having made the decisions described above, proper and timely preparation for Holy Week is essential not only for ensuring all the necessary stuff is in the right place at the right time, but also to ensure that the ministry team themselves can exude something of the reflective and contemplative spirit that is essential in guiding others through this most profound of journeys. There is no substitute for doing this practical task early on, thereby allowing the week itself to unfold in as unstressful manner as possible. Figure 7 is my genuine and unredacted checklist for Holy Week 2011, just as an example:

Figure 7: Sample Holy Week check-list

Holy Week and Easter 2011 Check list
Some time in Passion Week
KM take to Methodist Church on Tuesday evening – 50 palms, the Forthampton Processional Cross, Orders of Service for Palm Sunday, her cassock, surplice and cope
Palm Sunday
Take in morning: 30 palms for Forth – CFM 15 palms for Deerhurst – TC and 30 for Tredington
Monday of Holy Week
All: Penknives/New transfers for paschal candles as appropriate – get candles ready for Easter Day Leave dark red mass set in Apperley ready for Mon TC – After Deerhurst – Bring back candle to vicarage for 'sorting'
Tuesday of Holy Week
CEW – Set up new paschal candle at Forth before or after 7.30pm Mass

Wednesday of Holy Week

TC – During day or before Compline:	Take two folding chairs to Deerhurst Compline orders Add transfer and incense grains to the candle
Go to Chaceley and take Calvary Cross to Forthampton.	
Take to Forthampton:	Orders of Service for Good Friday Johannine Passion Narratives Set up altar of repose and table of the vestments Dark red set
In evening before Compline at Deerhurst:	Cranmerise the altar Set up Church for Maundy T other than 'valuables'
In evening after Compline – burn holy oils	Chairs, altar of repose, sanc lamps, bowl etc.

Maundy Thursday

Take to No. 4 in morning:	Oil stocks, white stole
After Chrism Mass – Collect from Longlevens:	'Filthy' white set for Maundy T Mass
In afternoon, take to Deerhurst:	Deerhurst White set (for Easter Day) Filthy White Set Sanctuary candles Orders of service and hymn sheets for MT evening Bowl, jug, towel Sheet of Watch readings Alb and 'sackcloth-white' stole Orders of service for Good F MP and Holy Sat MP A Bible

Set up:	Sanctuary Altar of repose – candles, corporal
Take on evening at 6.45pm:	Flask of warm water Pyx? Ciborium? Spare Chalice? Monster hosts (2)
Remember to set up:	Extra chalice and paten, with 25 extra hosts
Take back to vicarage:	Alb

Good Friday

Collect from Deerhurst:	Water carrier – to car Chairs – to car The Blessed Sacrament
Take to Forthampton:	Alb The Blessed Sacrament
After service:	Set up paschal candle

Holy Saturday

After Matins at Deerhurst:	Add transfer and incense grains to the paschal candle and take to vicarage Pack away altar of repose
Go to vigil at abbey:	Take Deerhurst's paschal candle

Easter Day

Take to Deerhurst:	Paschal candle
Take to Forthampton:	Flask of water Easter Day orders Switch of rosemary

Multiple churches: a case study from Severnside

One of the biggest challenges to observing a liturgically rich Holy Week in a rural benefice, as we have already noted, is the multiplicity of locations combined with the relatively small size of individual congregations and the lack of resources. What follows is a case study from the Severnside Benefice in which I sought to address these challenges in a creative way. As with all my examples it is unlikely this will map directly onto your context, but some of the methodology and ideas will, I hope, inspire you.

You will remember from a few pages earlier that part of my reasoning for choosing the locations for the Maundy Thursday and Good Friday liturgies was about the proximity of the two churches to each other. I had spent several years reflecting on the challenges multiple buildings present to keeping the Triduum. As we noted earlier, most of the liturgical manuals expect a congregation to inhabit the same space throughout the Great Three Days, experiencing the desolation of the space being stripped on Maundy Thursday evening, inhabiting that empty space through Good Friday and then rejoicing in entering back into the same space at Easter and finding it bedecked with flowers and finery. I wanted to try to carry people on that journey but nonetheless to make use of several buildings on the way. How to do that? And how, alongside that, to utilize all the wonderful symbology of the Triduum, including the procession of the Sacrament to a place of 'Gethsemane repose' on the Thursday night and distribute that same Sacrament the following afternoon as part of the Liturgy, even though the same building wasn't being used. How could I square this circle?

My solution was to invent a liturgical occasion to bridge the gap. I decided to connect the two churches physically, practically, liturgically and symbolically and that we would do the 'full works' on Maundy Thursday evening, including reserving the Sacrament at an altar of repose away from the main sanctuary of the church, and keep a Watch. The next day I would clear my diary for the whole morning, and walk, carrying the Sacrament, from the venue of the Thursday evening liturgy to the venue of the Good Friday liturgy. This would not only ensure the day was dedicated to reflection, but also make something rather more liturgical out of what would otherwise be a practical necessity to move the Sacrament in advance of the Good Friday liturgy. By doing something ritually symbolic, the two worship spaces, though separated by several miles of geography, would be connected by me, by the same ciborium and Sacrament, and I hoped by several of the worshipping congregation who might choose to undertake this walk with me.

I acknowledge there are some idiosyncrasies with this idea. A Procession of the Blessed Sacrament is no part of the traditional Liturgy of Good Friday. I needed to decide whether or not this would be a formal Procession and I decided that it would not. While a formal and ritualized carrying of the Sacrament has an honoured place on Maundy Thursday evening, as it does on days such as Corpus Christi, this seems somewhat incongruous on a day of mourning and reflection. For that reason I decided the procession would be much more of a quiet reflective walk. Because the churches are some way apart it would take several hours to undertake this journey and so for practical reasons too much paraphernalia would also be unhelpful. A quiet, stately walk through the countryside of the benefice in company, but with loud and enthusiastic conversation discouraged, and people given the option to join me for the entire journey or just a short part of it, seemed the best way to go. Other clergy in the benefice took turns to physically bear the Sacrament, which remained in its veiled ciborium from the night before. The priest carrying the Sacrament wore a red stole and the plain wooden processional cross was carried in front of the group in turn by lay members of the party.

A bit of analysis identified there were two churches that were the appropriate distance from Deerhurst for this to work, but also had the appropriate layout internally for the Good Friday liturgy to work well: Chaceley and Forthampton. To walk to Chaceley from Deerhurst would take pretty much precisely the amount of time we had to spare. Forthampton was some distance further away, but it occurred to me that if we crossed the river by boat the timings would work. By befriending a friendly member of the Sailing Club and organizing for him to attend us with a rowing boat after morning prayer on Good Friday, one year the Sacrament crossed the river by boat!

Crossing the river on Good Friday 2011

To further connect the two liturgical arenas, Good Friday began with the heavily truncated service of morning prayer suggested in *Common Worship: Daily Prayer* for use during the Triduum (CW: DP, p. xx). While truncating the Office in this way is not mandatory during the Triduum, it certainly lends a starkness and austerity to the experience and the notes in CW: DP are clear and helpful. So we gathered back in Deerhurst, where the Sacrament was still reserved in the side chapel with a white light burning beside it as it had been when people left in silence the night before. We gathered, however, not with the Sacrament but in the empty, stripped sanctuary, to quietly say morning prayer. At the end of that short service, with no ceremony, we moved to the altar of repose, I put on a red stole, picked up the ciborium and, preceded by the processional cross, walked out of the church. Once the Sacrament was underway, a churchwarden blew out the candle and stripped the altar of repose. An identical altar of repose was set up in the destination church, with a white sanctuary lamp waiting to be lit when we arrived. In both instances the altar of repose was a temporary installation, simply a table with a white tablecloth thrown over it and one of those seven-day candles that are often used in hanging lamps.

The connecting of the worship spaces in this way thus had a number of effects. First there was a liturgical point being made: that symbolically and liturgically, this is the same space. By physically moving the Sacrament in a deliberate, slow and measured way, something that

Good Friday walk 2012

could have been very utilitarian became an act of worship in itself. Taking the time to try to make the two altars of repose look as identical as possible further reinforced this. Inviting people to walk with me not only made the journey itself into a communal act of prayer and fellowship, but undoubtedly increased attendance on Good Friday. By making it clear the walk was optional, and that people could join and leave at any point, flexibility was built in. Probably about half the people walked the entire way with me, while a similar number either did the first half-hour or so from Deerhurst, or joined the walk on the other side of the river. Doing something that was seen as a little bit 'quirky' lent a certain publicity to the day which I think also had an effect on numbers. The process of carrying the Sacrament also provided the opportunity for informal conversation about sacramental theology more generally before, after and to a certain extent during the walk, and so was a teaching moment. Finally, the public nature of this process meant the whole event was an opportunity for mission and evangelism.

Multiple churches: other possibilities

It would be possible to do something similar to my Severnside case study at other points during Holy Week. Depending on the configuration of your benefice, and the results of your ecclesiological and liturgical analysis, it would be possible to turn the Palm Sunday procession into a journey between two buildings. With the right geography, it might also be possible to move from the Maundy Thursday building to the Good Friday one in the evening of Maundy Thursday, creating something of an extended procession of the Blessed Sacrament to the altar of repose in a different building. I also imagine the Good Friday liturgy being split, with the Liturgy of the Word taking place in one building followed by an extensive Procession of the Cross to another village where the veneration of the Cross might happen. This opens up creative possibilities for ecumenical liturgy.

Hitting the key theological truths: a case study from Tidenham

In another sort of book I would go into much more detail about each of the liturgies of this wonderful week. Space precludes that here, and there are several recent and good liturgical manuals which offer a range of liturgical instruction in a broadly modern catholic style. In closing this section on Holy Week, I simply return to the repeated appeal of this book: the key to success in liturgical ministry in the rural context is to know very clearly what the key theological truths are that we want to communicate and then be selective about the liturgical symbols that are utilized. In a situation where we can probably only manage with what we can fit into our car, prioritization is essential. Washing three sets of feet is far easier than washing

12 sets of feet if we need to bring folding chairs, jugs and hot water with us. The theological truth we communicate is about humility and the servant nature of the ministry of Christ. To even wash one set of feet will communicate this powerfully. That might be the priority on Maundy Thursday, particularly if there will not be a reception of the Eucharist on Good Friday. Feet might trump the reservation of the Sacrament if only one or the other is manageable. This is precisely what happens in Tidenham. The tradition of the parish is such that receiving the reserved Sacrament on Good Friday would be theologically challenging and so the foot washing is prioritized. Three or four sets of feet are washed, and then at the end of the Maundy Thursday liturgy the ablutions are performed as normal and after the post-communion prayer the sanctuary is stripped. Instead of a movement to an altar of repose, the congregation remains in the nave of the church, the lights are dimmed and a corporate silence is held, the focus being the stripped sanctuary contrasted with the bowls, jugs and towels from the foot washing which remain prominently visible. People are then invited to leave in silence when they wish. A subtly different theological truth is held here: that of the curious and uncomfortable tension between the self-giving love of Christ and the inability of his people to watch with him.

Easter Day

The same principles apply on Easter Day. Which liturgical symbols are going to speak most clearly and articulately of the Resurrection? Undoubtedly predominant among these liturgical symbols, excepting the Eucharist itself, are the paschal candle and the water of baptism. Recognizing that in many rural contexts this might mean the purchase and setting up of a dozen candles, and the utilizing of the same number of fonts, in rural churches a decision will need to be made about the priorities. For several years I prioritized the renewal of baptismal vows in Severnside, which provoked some robust conversation about the decorating, or otherwise, of the fonts! Transporting warm water around the benefice in huge vacuum flasks was certainly a challenge and led me to discover which of my fonts could actually hold water. Renewing baptismal vows on this, of all days, is certainly powerful and CW: TS provides a handful of different ways in which this might be done, including within the Vigil service, at a stand-alone service at dawn, or during a mid-morning service which may or may not be Eucharistic. When it is possible to baptize someone, so much the better! It is instructive to note that throughout CW: TS the two dominant symbols of the paschal candle and the water of baptism are encouraged, regardless of the form of service that might take place. Parishes which have a tradition of an open-air service at dawn might well be encouraged by the provision (p. 400) for a very informal act of worship which still includes the 'Easter Light' and the reaffirmation of baptismal vows which 'might be done with whatever water is naturally available.'

Something which works particularly well in multi-parochial benefices is the provision for 'welcoming the Easter Candle into Church' (CW: TS, p. 418). If a benefice-wide vigil is held, representatives from each local congregation could be invited to light a candle or lamp from the paschal candle at the end of that service, or indeed light their paschal candle. At the beginning of each local Easter service the following morning, that same representative could bring in the light (keeping the candle burning all night is not required!) from the vestry or main door. Again, here's a simple way to link each local congregation with the wider benefice or deanery.

Some imaginative liturgy focusing on the Easter Garden is also provided (p. 419). In a post-coronavirus world where the importance of open-air worship has been re-emphasized, there might be some particular work to be done developing this material. If the Alleluia was buried in the churchyard on the Sunday before Lent, it could also be 'discovered' by the children at this point and either brought back into church or displayed at the Easter Garden.

Joining the threads

We have noted that, unlike the Advent and Christmas cycle, the observation of the Easter cycle emphasizes the systematic unfolding of a long story. That story is at its most focused during Holy Week, but it begins on Ash Wednesday and continues until Pentecost. There are different ecclesiological emphases here and the relationship between the liturgy and the local is markedly distinct. In the heart of the season, the challenge for the local leaders of worship is about telling the story in a way that is both coherent and consistent, while managing the expectations of a number of buildings and communities. We have reflected that perhaps there are two key moments during this cycle where the local is at its most important: Mothering Sunday and Easter. We have noticed the possibility of telling the story in an extended journey through the benefice, identifying the geographical locations which will speak most eloquently of the theological truths that are being described. One particular example, Maundy Thursday, has opened up the potential for uniting worship centres in a way that is liturgical, recognizes the local and invites engagement in the story. We have reminded ourselves again of the importance of identifying the key theological truths and structuring our practical preparations around helping those truths to sing, as eloquently as possible, in the place where we are.

5

The Agricultural Year:
Rural Festivals

You crown the year with your goodness

CW preserves the Collect for Harvest Thanksgiving, with its
address to the God who 'crown[s] the year with [his] goodness
and ... give[s] us the fruits of the earth in their season'. The
Collect draws its inspiration from Psalm 65, and the prayer
itself originates in the 1989 South African Prayer Book (Bradshaw, p. 222). CW notes that 'Harvest Thanksgiving may be
celebrated on Sunday and may replace the provision for that
day, provided it does not supersede any Principal Feast or
Festival' (CW, p. 447). The fact that a celebration of thanksgiving for the fruits of the land and the sea is deemed significant
enough to displace the Lectionary provision for a Sunday is
evidence enough of the importance that the Church of England
chooses to place on worship that acknowledges and honours
the natural providence of creation. The liturgical revisions of
recent decades have enhanced and developed the provision,
creating a cycle of what might be deemed 'agricultural festivals'
interwoven with the Sunday and Saints Day cycles, resulting in
a distinctive Church of England calendar which speaks to the
sort of relationship between community, land, congregation
and faith that we have been unfolding.

Provision of an agricultural nature is not unique to the
Church of England. Many denominations and liturgical traditions note the distinctive themes of growth, and the call to be
fruitful rather than barren. Elliott notes that after the Feast
of the Trinity, 'the year of the church settles into the time of

growth, the Season of the year, sometimes called "Ordinary Time"' (Elliott, p. 167). The use of green as the default liturgical colour is often referenced for its symbolism as the colour of growth and the natural world.

Kennedy with Haselock, introducing the Lectionary material themed around Creation, stated in 2006:

> [T]here has been a widespread conviction that creation has not been a strong focus in recent liturgical revision. For example, the lack of lectionary material on creation in the Revised Common Lectionary has long been noted. In some ways, this is not surprising, as the lectionary takes as its starting point the gospel reading, and it is a simple fact that the Gospels do not include much material on specifically creation-related themes. Or at least, where there are references to the natural world in the Gospels, for example in the parables, the overriding theme is something broader, such as Jesus' teaching about the kingdom of God. It was for this reason that the Liturgical Commission departed from the RCL provision for the Second Sunday before Lent in order to incorporate creation-based lections and Collects for that day. (Kennedy with Haselock, pp. 146–7)

When Kennedy with Haselock were writing in 2008, they were commentating on the provision in CW: TS in the section entitled Seasons and Festivals of the Agricultural Year. Here the provision in the Core CW volume is augmented with a suite of resources covering:

- Creation
- Plough Sunday
- Rogationtide
- Lammastide
- Harvest Thanksgiving

Beyond this development however, work on developing a season of 'Creationtide' was bubbling away. This has grown in both prominence and significance over recent years as issues of preservation and conservation of the natural environment, ecology and responsible stewardship have established themselves as highly significant.

In addition to these seasons there is a far less formally bounded 'summer season': a time which instinctively we imagine begins somewhere around the time of public exams and the ending of the school term, ends somewhere in mid-September and which is associated with a change to the normal routines of many people. In some parishes this might be marked by a subtle change in the worship schedule, the absence of a formal choir during school holidays, increased visitors in some holiday hotspots, and for many the peak of the wedding season. In the Severnside Benefice, with a fine village team in Apperley, it mapped roughly onto the cricket season! All of this is subtle, and hard to pin down, but there is something of this 'English summer' period which might have liturgical as well as other implications.

The focus of this chapter is therefore on how we might navigate the voluminous provision, and how the keeping of some of these observations, ancient or modern, might be another piece in the jigsaw puzzle of our rural theology and ecclesiology.

Jones and Martin, in their biblical analysis of agricultural society, point to the way in which the rhythms of farming profoundly influence worship in the Bible:

> Many of the biblical feasts were linked to events in the farming calendar. This linked everyone into relationship with the natural world, to renew a grasp of food, landscape, air and space as gifts and to relate these gifts and themselves to the creation. First, of course, church and farmers need to relearn this and lead the way (p. 116).

The careful biblical analysis in their volume is well worth reading. Connections are drawn between festivals and Feasts that develop through the pages of the Scripture and the account of Creation, thus hallowing 'a basic cycle of night following day to enable a balance of work, rest and refreshment. Festivals, sabbath and rotating the land are key principles'. Feasts, in the

Old Testament, are communal and symbolic, thus, 'they put in perspective human reality: sin, judgement, forgiveness and they cultivate an attitude of praise and thanksgiving in sharing God's blessings' (p. 54).

New and innovative material is emerging all the time, but it is worth noting two resources which have been published during the time I have been writing this book. The first, a Church of England Liturgical Commission publication, *A Time for Creation* (TFC) gathers together all the scattered broadly 'creation-flavoured' material into one slim paperback volume, augmented with some new compositions. The introduction to this volume strongly echoes the thoughts I offered at the beginning of this book about the symbolism of rural churches being 'seeds in holy ground'. The well-known extract from Julian of Norwich concerning the hazelnut is quoted:

> [H]e showed me a little thing, the size of a hazelnut, on the palm of my hand, round like a ball. I looked at it thoughtfully and wondered, 'what is this?' And the answer came, 'it is all that is made.' I marvelled that it continued to exist and did not suddenly disintegrate; it was so small. And again my mind supplied the answer, 'it exists, both now and forever, because God loves it.' In short, everything owes its existence to the love of God. In this 'little thing' I saw three truths. The first is that God made it; the second is that God loves it; and the third is that God sustains it. (TFC, p. 5, quoting Julian of Norwich, *Revelations of Divine Love*, Chapter 5)

TFC is reasonably inexpensive so could be purchased in bulk for churches. It is also available as an e-book, and the vast majority of the material already exists on the website.

The second notable recent publication is Chris Thorpe's *Ploughshares and First Fruits*, which comprises a suite of ready-made liturgies aimed particularly at rural church communities: '*Ploughshares and First Fruits* explores traditional agricultural feasts, new countryside festivals, Saints days and themes to bring rural communities together in worship' (p. ix).

Although not all the festivals provided for are rural in nature, they are deliberately framed for a rural community and the book is the output of 10 years of ministry in three rural parishes in Shropshire (Thorpe, p. x). Some of the ecclesiology that underpins *Ploughshares* will be explored below.

For the final time in this volume let us glance through our analytical lenses, and discern how the agricultural festivals might add another layer of revelation to our rural Christian experience.

A glance through the ecclesiological lens

We have noted that locality brings into relief certain of the truths of God, and of our salvation. St Paul reminded the people of God in Corinth that there is one body with many members, and each member finds a particular place within the body which is neither more nor less important than any other, but is nonetheless distinct (1 Cor. 12.12–27). This truth holds both for individual Christians within the body, and also individual communities. Rural churches proclaim clearly, visibly and confidently a set of truths that are in fact universal. Proximity to the countryside naturally leads to the preferment of a set of agricultural themes:

> Some communities, both urban and rural, will wish, because of their proximity to the countryside, to make explicit in their liturgical programmes the importance of these celebrations as a matter of mission and affirmation of the agricultural industries and communities. (Kennedy with Haselock, p. 148)

Honey and Thistles (pp. 43–52) draws out what some of these biblical themes are:

- An awareness that the land, and its health, can parallel our human relationships, reminding us of God's demand that his people be fair in their distribution of the land (Num. 26.52–56)

- The recollection that the sort of relationship that God calls us to is a covenant (Gen. 9.12, 15)
- That attention to the poor is a commandment (Deut. 15.4)
- That God instituted Sabbath rest and restraint (Ex. 20.8–11; Deut. 5.12–15) and that Jubilee is also something on which God insists (Lev. 25.8–13)
- That food is important both practically and symbolically. The authors note that the account of the feeding of the five thousand appears in every gospel (Matt. 14.13–21; Mark 6.31–44; Luke 9.12–17; John 6.1–14) and that, alongside manifold other references to food, meals, and hospitality, the Lord's Prayer contains the petition about daily bread (Matt. 6.9–13; Luke 11.2–4)

All these interlocking biblical themes might be discovered at the deep root level of a rural community's ecclesiology. Perhaps the reminder of the divine institution of the Sabbath, and the importance of not trying to work every hour of every day, or repeating tasks dozens of times in each small parish might be an important one to remember. The concept of keeping the fallow is probably something that multi-parochial benefices would do well to revisit.

TFC provides a set of references from the tradition, and particularly emphasizes that it is a Christian imperative to pray with, as well as for, creation. Tertullian, Gregory of Nazianzus and St Francis of Assisi are all referenced as we are reminded that there is a distinct and honoured tradition of creation itself being both capable of 'groaning in travail' (Rom. 8.22) and also offering praise to its creator (Ps. 148). This important theme of creation both suffering and praising, and the associated interconnectivity between what humanity might be doing and how that relates to the rest of creation might be something to which rural communities are particularly attuned.

Ploughshares offers a distinct ecclesiology of the rural church based on identifying festival occasions as key to the mission of such communities. Thorpe argues that since the big festival occasions are when most people come to church in a rural

community, they are really where the majority of resources
need to be placed. He describes this kind of ecclesiology as:

> ... a mission led response ... [o]ffering stepping-stones,
> opening connections between the heart of our own lives
> and the heart of faith. It contains resources for hard-pressed
> church leaders, whether clergy or not, to enable churches
> to reconnect with the local community. It seeks to draw the
> occasional visitor, who might attend church at Christmas,
> Easter, Harvest and Remembrance, to attend on a more
> regular basis, perhaps at a monthly 'festival'. (Thorpe, p. ix)

This ecclesiology is interesting, and proceeds on the basis of
identifying one service a month that will be badged as a 'festival'
and act a bit like a shopfront for the parish. He provides a
fully worked out set of liturgical resources for a 12-month
cycle of such festivals, drawing some material from CW: TS,
but ranging more widely and imaginatively. It is a distinct and
interesting ecclesiology which, on reflection, might work well
in tandem with the sort of ecclesiology I develop of recognizing
the parallels between rural communities and monastic communities. In religious communities, the cycle of prayer is simple
and predictable, a quiet, faithful, daily recitation of familiar
Offices, mostly attended by the professed members of the community. However, when feast days or Sundays occur there is
often a brief flurry of more active, colourful and elaborate liturgy. The congregation might be swelled by many visitors or
parishioners. Liturgical paraphernalia might emerge, incense
might be used, with a significantly enhanced musical repertoire.
I wonder whether we find in a book such as Thorpe's another
useful building block for our rural ecclesiology? If we do look
at our scattered rural communities through the lens of the
religious community, might we see two interconnected cycles:
the faithful, unceasing, probably fairly simple and predictable
offering of daily and weekly worship, attended by a handful
of people, then enhanced by greater attendance and the flashes
of colour, ceremony and innovation that herald the coming of
what Thorpe refers to as 'festivals'? He also makes some inter-

esting comments about the nature of sacred space, symbolic action and communication, which further enhance our rural ecclesiology.

A glance through the liturgical-theological lens

For the rural church with an ambition to take its liturgical life seriously, the cycles of the liturgical year bear a natural and welcome familiarity. After all, the fundamental cycles of all liturgical time are the day, the week and the year. As we say our prayers we trace the passage of morning and evening, we tread the path from Sunday to Sunday, passing each week through the day of crucifixion and the day of resting in the tomb before beginning another day of Resurrection. Our annual calendars, both of movable and fixed Feasts and fasts, carry us from Advent to Advent, through the darkest part of the year to the balmy days of midsummer and back again. Jones and Martin recognize this rhythm, this heartbeat, which pulses through all Christian liturgical worship; a pulse at its most audible in the countryside:

> The creator set in motion a basic cycle of night following day to enable a balance of work, rest and refreshment. Festivals, sabbath and rotating the land are key principles ... [in the Old Testament these feasts] put in perspective human reality: sin, judgement, forgiveness and they cultivate an attitude of praise and thanksgiving in sharing God's blessings. (p. 54)

A warning is sometimes sounded of the dangers of too much focus on creation as a theme in Christian worship. There is the risk of worship losing something of its doctrinal groundedness. Language of creation, when not married confidently to the Incarnation, the atonement, salvation, and the doctrine of the Trinity, can run the risk of deifying almost everything. For the Church of England, whose doctrine is traditionally found within its liturgical formulae, this is a warning worth taking seriously. Casting an eye over any piece of liturgy once drafted to ensure it is indeed a recognizably Christian prayer or act of worship is no bad routine to adopt. CW: TS notes, 'the same Scriptures bear witness to concerns about the idolatry of fertility cults and the worship of created things rather than the creator' (p. 596). TFC also recognizes this danger, and confronts it head on. When discussing the (really very new) concept of a month-long autumn season of Creation, the Liturgical Commission notes, 'the Feast of the Holy Cross, coming midway through September, also presents an opportunity to reflect on the cosmic significance of the cross and to give some welcome Christological grounding to the season' (TFC, p. 8).

Agricultural festivals

CW: TS includes a section entitled 'Seasons and Festivals of the Agricultural Year'. This provides, sequentially, resources for: Creation, Plough Sunday, Rogationtide, Lammastide, and Harvest Thanksgiving, together with some prayer for use in Times of Agricultural Crisis (pp. 594–5). In the following section we will consider these resources briefly, noting where other advice exists, and reflecting on possibilities of each occasion. We will leave Creation until last, however, and then lead into some reflections on open-air worship and the summer season.

Plough Sunday

Although a relatively recent reintroduction into the formal liturgical material of the Church of England, the English tradition of marking the return to the fields after the Christmas festivities goes back a long way. The religious observance of the First Sunday after Epiphany for this purpose seems to be Victorian in origin, drawing on earlier practice. Kennedy with Haselock observe that the practice, 'witnesses to an instinct that at the start of the calendar year we ask for God's blessing on the work of the year ahead. The plough continues to be a powerful symbol of preparation and of the potential of the Earth's fruitfulness and fertility to sustain us in life' (p. 153).

While the BCP provision for the First Sunday after Epiphany has a gentle 'holy family' feel to it, with the gospel reading of the finding of the child Jesus in the temple and his obedience to his parents (Luke 2.41–52), CW prefers the Feast of the Baptism of Christ and provides quite a lot of liturgical material for this. This makes it trickier to observe Plough Sunday and for that reason there is encouragement, particularly from Kennedy with Haselock, to be imaginative in terms of where in January this rather lovely tradition might be maintained. In rural communities where there is a great deal of agriculture practised, consulting the local farmers might be the first step to identifying when and where a Plough service might be best held. One option might be to lean into the theme of returning to work in the new year and create a kind of New Year's service, drawing in some of the resources from CW: TS, pp. 105–15 which includes the material for the Renewal of the Covenant, itself Methodist in origin. Returning to our conversation about what to do with the few days after Christmas, one of those Sundays might suit this type of service which would focus on Thanksgiving, re-commitments and new beginnings, and into which some focus on the return of life to the earth might fit quite well.

The heart of the CW: TS resources are two rather fine prayers of blessing: for the Plough itself and for seed. By implication where possible there ought to be a physical ploughing implement present, as well as some actual seed. There is potential for using a traditional plough where one might still exist, but the real-life connections might be made stronger by gathering outside around a piece of modern farm equipment. If the Sundays following Christmas already feel too congested (a real danger with the CW calendar) there would seem to be no reason not to observe this occasion midweek, which opens up huge potential for a rather exciting school service, perhaps with a field trip to the local farm, or inviting a farmer to bring their modern plough to the school gates. There are creative opportunities here to tie this religious observance with the curriculum, perhaps making connections with geography, environmental

studies or indeed issues around cookery, diet and food pro-
duction. TFC and *Ploughshares* both include suggestions and
material for this occasion.

Rogationtide

We tend to think of Rogationtide services and processions,
with idyllic images of beating of the bounds, as quintessentially
English. The modern observance is Roman Catholic in origin.
In both the traditional and modern Roman calendar, the roga-
tions are prescribed:

> The Rogation Ember days were traditionally observed on the
> Feast of St Mark, April 25, and on the Monday, Tuesday
> and Wednesday before the Ascension of Our Lord. On these
> days it was customary to pray for the needs of all people,
> and especially for the productivity of the Earth and human
> labour, rendering thanks to our bountiful Lord for his good-
> ness revealed in creation ... Obviously this intensive interces-
> sion and thanksgiving responds to times either of planting or
> harvesting vintage in the rural societies in both hemispheres.
> (Elliot, p. 164)

The tone of the Rogation processions used to be penitential,
and indeed in the traditional rite the service is celebrated in
purple vestments. The modern Roman Rite, and CW, suggest
the use of white instead, emphasizing the prevailing Easter
tone and preferring themes of thanksgiving and hope over penitence. It is interesting, however, that the tone of penitence has
not completely disappeared even in CW, with the introduction
to the confession referencing both the weariness of the earth
itself, and our complicity:

> Let us ask God to have mercy on our tired land,
> and to prosper the work of our soiled hands.
> Let us ask God to forgive our delusion of self-sufficiency

so that we may praise him for his provision and goodness
(CW: TS, p. 609)

CW: TS provides resources for a procession which might be
either 'the traditional beating of the bounds or a specified procession in part of the parish' (p. 614). There are all sorts of
imaginative opportunities here. First it ought to be remembered
that the traditional Rogation Days are in fact the Monday,
Tuesday and Wednesday following the Sixth Sunday of Easter
so there is nothing to prevent processions, walks and services
on these midweek days. Where appropriate schools within the
benefice could be involved in beating the bounds, either of part
of the parish or of their own sites. Depending on the geography,
processions could move from one church to another, either on
the Sunday or through the week. It is deep in the tradition for
processions at this time to move from one church to the other
(Elliot, p. 164).

The material in CW: TS includes some traditional language
provision drawn from the Litany, together with a contemporary translation of those texts. The Litany, in either its BCP
or CW form, is a magnificent liturgical text and well worth
rediscovering. It has the great benefit of being easy for the congregation to join in, with only a few changes in the simple
congregational response. It could easily also be sung by one
confident singer chanting the ministerial texts. There is a
wealth of hymnody picking up on very similar themes. The
'Lament for a time of global environmental and climate crisis'
in TFC is a rather fine text which could be dropped into a
procession, complementing the Litany, and perhaps some less
formal hymn singing. There are several other nuggets in the
same section of TFC (pp. 44–48) which could be selected from
as appropriate. Benefices on the sea coast, or through which
significant waterways run, might find the 'prayer for the waters
and the seas' useful, and the 'act of commitment for the care of
creation' would be a fine conclusion to a processional liturgy
in any rural context.

Returning to the conversation of Chapter 4 around which
buildings are used for which services during the Easter cycle,

there is also opportunity here for a benefice-wide five-day cycle of worship. Perhaps the service on the Sixth Sunday of Easter (often still referred to in rural communities as Rogation Sunday) could be a united benefice service, with a procession to another church at the end of it. Successive churches, schools, homes or farms could be visited on the intervening days, culminating in another benefice service in a final church building on Ascension Day. The time of the year lends itself to this kind of event, when evening worship is more likely to be attractive.

Kennedy with Haselock have excellent advice for the keeping of Rogationtide: 'two major rogation themes [are]: prayer that the fruits of the earth may be given in due season, and petition for human work and industry' (p. 155). The weaving together of Creation and Easter themes during this week is encouraged, with 'Alleluia, alleluia, hearts to heaven and voices raise' offered as an example of an ideal hymn for the occasion, containing as it does a mixture of agrarian and paschal imagery. George Herbert's elucidation of the four principal benefits of holding a procession is also recalled: blessing God for the crops, the themes of justice related to maintaining boundaries, charity or love in the companionship of the journey, and mercy in caring for the poor (Kennedy with Haselock, pp. 156–7, referring to chapter 25 of George Herbert's *A Priest to the Temple*).

Ploughshares contains a fully worked out service entitled 'Daring to Ask' which draws on a lot of the same suggestions as in the Plough Sunday service in the same volume including a blessing of the soil and the seed but not, interestingly, a procession. There is express encouragement to involve local farmers or growers in the service (Thorpe, pp. 88–94).

Finally, it is worth remembering the page of specific resources for the Rogation Days in CW: DP (p. 537) with which the daily Office can be augmented. There are special antiphons for the Benedictus and Magnificat, a selection of three Collects, and suggestions for alternative canticles. Canon B5 would provide sufficient authority for using some of this material on the Fifth Sunday of Easter as well as on the succeeding three weekdays, where appropriate.

There is space and flexibility enough, in the CW resources and in the tradition, for a combination of themes to be drawn together over Rogationtide. Alongside the opportunities for strengthening a united benefice or Team identity through the imaginative use of processions and foci on boundaries, other themes might well include a strain of penitence, drawing on some of the environmental prayers in TFC, as well as thanksgiving and blessing. The relationship of humanity to the rest of creation is undoubtably a complex one, containing significant abuses as well as real moments of joyful thanksgiving, and it does no harm to recognize that at this time of year.

Lammastide

One of the curiosities of the BCP is that although very little seasonal material is provided within the texts of the Eucharistic rite or the Offices, the calendar itself, found nestling at the front of the book, lists a number of observations including days of fasting and feasts. Among them is found, on the first day of August, 'Lammas Day'. It is intriguing to reflect on why certain holy days were retained when the BCP calendar was constructed. Lammas Day is one of six feast days retained in the month of August. The origin is pre-Reformation, and Kennedy with Haselock provide useful background (p. 161). It is an explicitly Eucharistic observation, a 'loaf mass' offered as thanksgiving for the first-fruits of the harvest and CW: TS and TFC reproduce the same material, which provides for the Presentation of the Lammas Loaf at the beginning of the service:

> Brothers and sisters in Christ, the people of God in ancient times presented to the Lord an offering of first-fruits as a sign of their dependence upon God for their daily bread. At this Lammastide, we bring a newly baked loaf as our offering in thanksgiving to God for his faithfulness (CW: TS, p. 619).

A verse from the sixth chapter of St John's gospel then connects the tradition of first-fruits with the Christological concept of Jesus as bread of life.

The immediate challenge is that 1 August will rarely fall on a Sunday, and the proximity of the Transfiguration may on occasion produce a conflict. Local custom should be the guiding factor here, and it would not seem unreasonable to, on occasion, translate the Lammas observation to the final Sunday of July, or to allow it to coexist with Transfiguration. There are interesting parallels between the revelation of the full nature of Christ and reflections on how something as apparently simple and domestic as bread can speak to us of divine providence. Alternatively, where holiday patterns permit, perhaps a midweek event during August might be possible. See below for more reflections on the possibilities of the 'summer season' and open-air worship.

CW: TS is acutely aware of the risk of confusing the symbol of the Lammas Loaf with the Eucharistic Host, and stresses in a note that worship leaders must take great care the two do not become confused. There is provision for the Lammas Loaf to be used later in the service as the Eucharistic element, but the two actions: the first the Presentation of the Lammas Loaf, and the second the offertory, must be kept distinct. Some churches will be attracted by the idea of baking a special loaf which is ceremonially presented at the beginning of the service and then later used as the Eucharistic bread, making all sorts of connections with the offering back to God of the gifts he gives to us. Others, particularly those who would struggle with seemly distribution of 'real' bread, might choose to keep the two entirely separate, perhaps leaving the Lammas Loaf on a table at the head of the nave throughout the service.

Ploughshares takes a confident step away from the advice of CW: TS and provides a fully worked out liturgy which includes the ceremonial (though not sacramental) breaking and reception of the Lammas Loaf towards the end of the service:

Sharing the Lammas Loaf

The Lammas loaf is broken and given to a child to distribute to everyone present.

We eat and reflect in silence. (Thorpe, p. 143)

This is undoubtedly a more confusing ritual act, and will require considerably more teaching and explanation, but that does not necessarily mean it might not be appropriate in certain contexts. There are honourable traditions of the distribution of blessed, but not consecrated, bread and this service has more of an *agape* feel to it. Caution must undoubtedly be exercised in the preparation of such a service to ensure the congregation understand clearly they are not participating in a Eucharist, and neither has anything like consecration taken place. Writing this chapter, as I am, at the very beginning of the third national lockdown, in January 2021, I am acutely aware there is a larger conversation going on at the moment about the differences and the relationship between the consecration of the Eucharistic elements, and any other reception of food and drink in a ceremonial or fellowship ritual. The edges of our Eucharistic doctrine have been impact tested over the past year or so in a way which has been quite painful for many, but will hopefully result in a refreshed exploration of, and engagement with, the sacramental life of the Church of England. It is to be hoped a place will be found for non-sacramental expressions of fellowship, clearly demarcated from the sacraments, and it is possible that occasions such as Lammastide might give context to this conversation.

Harvest Thanksgiving

The Harvest Thanksgiving, or Festival, is the most embedded of the agricultural festivals, and least needs to be said about it. There are well-established traditional patterns in very many places. Kennedy with Haselock suggest there are four major traditions currently in operation: Harvest Evensong, a parish Eucharist, an all-age service, and variations on a Harvest Songs of Praise. Many parishes might offer more than one of these. We are urged not to forget the rather lovely 'bringing forward of the symbols of the harvest' liturgy provided by CW: TS (p. 629). It takes the form of a litany, sequentially calling forward 'the harvest of the cornfields ... The harvest of roots ... The harvest of seeds for next year's crops...' CW: TS positions it as part of the offertory at a Eucharist, but it could just as easily be adapted to form the central act of a Service of the Word, or perhaps the introductory part of an evening Songs of Praise. In the same bank of resources there are two comprehensive sets of intercessions, both of which address issues of poverty, starvation and the economic influences upon agriculture. There is also a rather fine thanksgiving which might be used in a similar way to those described above in the Rogation section, perhaps as a conclusion to an open-air act of worship, or a procession outdoors at the end of a harvest service.

CW: DP has a page of resources for the daily Office (p. 536) which could either be used on a single occasion, perhaps flavouring the Office on Harvest Sunday, or could be used regularly (though perhaps not daily) throughout Creationtide.

The key thing to mention here is that we need to note the significant additional resourcing around the season of Creation, most of which did not exist at the point where CW: TS or CW: DP were published. Rather than Harvest standing alone, there is now explicit encouragement for communities to treat the whole of the early autumn as a quasi-season, and we will go on to consider that in the next section.

Creationtide

A focus on creation has an unsettled recent history in the Church of England. The ASB calendar began not with Advent Sunday but with the Ninth Sunday before Christmas, in mid-October. The first couple of weeks focused on the creation of the world, and then the subsequent Fall. There were many reasons for moving away from this model as the calendar was revised. Mid-October is not a good time to begin a sequence of thematic preaching, and the Ninth Sunday before Christmas frequently fell during half term, thus meaning the theme of creation would be missed by many. The Common Worship Lectionary (itself an edited version of the Revised Common Lectionary) moves the theme of creation to the Second Sunday before Lent, and indeed the Collect provided for that Sunday in CW is the Collect composed for the ASB for the Ninth Sunday before Christmas. The creation theme works better here than it did in mid-October, falling at a time of year where there are green shoots and early spring flowers emerging. A duo of Sundays thus lead up to the beginning of Lent, with creation themes on the Second Sunday followed by a Sunday heavily themed around the Transfiguration. There are still issues with the positioning of half term in some years.

Creationtide is not intended to replace the Second Sunday before Lent, though there is permission to divert from the Lectionary during Ordinary Time, so if a community is intending to throw a lot of resource behind an autumn season of Creation then there would be nothing wrong with replacing the readings on the couple of Sundays before Lent to avoid repetition. Rather than seeking to supersede the provision in the Lectionary, the real motivation behind the development of Creationtide is the acute awareness, growing steadily over the past 20 years, of the impact of humanity upon the natural environment and the importance of living harmoniously with creation.

TFC provides some history on the development of a season of creation. It traces the modern developments to the musings of the Ecumenical Patriarch in 1989, which might surprise some (TFC, p. 8). Most of the actual material in the book is not new, though a few pieces of liturgy are original compositions. What the book does very usefully is draw the scattered material together into a manageable volume, rationalize it and draw some of the themes together. Apart from the liturgy I have already drawn attention to, probably the most intriguing new composition is the set of thematic resources which is offered on pp. 76–9. Three possible sermon series are provided with themes, suggested Bible readings and some simple liturgical material. For those familiar with the sermon series suggestions in NPW the format will be familiar. What is innovative is that three 'strands' are provided, so that over a three-year cycle different themes can be explored. Each of the three strands provides a four-week lectionary and set of themes thus:

- Strand 1: Of Every Kind. A series focusing on the stages of agricultural farming: Sowing, Growing, Gathering, Treasuring.
- Strand 2: The Garden: The Spade, The Watering Can, The Basket, The Plate.
- Strand 3: Creation Emergency. This strand is the most explicitly focused on ecological and environmental issues. The four weeks are entitled Wonder, Abundance, Desolation, Restoration.

The first benefit of the most recent attempt at developing a structured focus on creation in the Church of England is the explicit connection between the season and Harvest Thanksgiving. The idea is that Harvest Thanksgiving falls at some point within the period between the beginning of September and the Feast of St Francis of Assisi, which are the suggested outer bounds of the season. There is no reason why the season could not be contracted or extended where locally appropriate. The second great benefit is that the entirety of the season should fall during school term time. The sermon series described above could readily be used as the structure for a month-long series of school assemblies, and could also inform children's ministry on Sundays. The month of themed preaching and worship could culminate in the Harvest Thanksgiving, or indeed the main service could kick off a month of reflection.

Many rural parishes will have been informally observing something like a season of Creation for many years. In Severnside I inherited a pattern of harvest festivals which ran over something like four weeks; some services traditionally taking place midweek and others on Sundays. Most of them had an associated harvest supper, and both schools were also in the habit of coming to church for their own harvest service. Thus

Flower Festival at Deerhurst

I had something like eight acts of worship which were harvest themed. What I did was to gently bracket all these services together by deciding to use the material for Harvest Thanksgiving or Creation from CW: TS at all CW Eucharists across the benefice over that period, and to use the CW: DP provision at daily morning and evening prayer two or three times a week. On any day where the weather permitted I said the daily Offices in the open air in the churchyard as well. None of this was particularly overt, but it had the effect of permeating the entire benefice in the language and theological themes contained within the liturgy. I also encouraged the harvest decorations to be left up for as long as possible. In Tidenham, Harvest itself is focused on a single Sunday, with a fairly traditional Eucharist at 9 o'clock which includes the bringing forward of the harvest gifts, followed by an all-age act of worship later in the morning, and a festival Songs of Praise service with refreshments in the evening. In many places, including both Severnside and Tidenham, harvest offerings are brought from homes and the schools and laid before the altar. Where security allows, it is lovely if the gifts can remain in place until the last service is completed at which point they can be boxed and taken to the distribution point. I personally have quite strong feelings about not placing too many things on the altar and favour the setting up of a low table in the sanctuary or chancel, on and around which gifts can be placed.

In terms of daily services during this season, TFC provides several fully worked out services including the daily Offices. Probably the best thing about these services is the rather lovely rendering of the Benedicite (TFC pp. 10–16). Where it is economically viable, purchasing half a dozen copies of TFC would allow a small midweek congregation to use the fully worked out services as the daily Office texts throughout the month. One curious decision of the Liturgical Commission, however, is to radically reduce the Scripture readings, providing brief gobbets in the style of the Roman Catholic Divine Office. If you use these orders of service any more regularly than once or twice, I would ignore that and continue to use the daily readings from a Bible, otherwise the daily diet of Scripture will be very meagre. Suggested seasonal psalms and canticles are all printed out in the text.

If you are searching for other resources, Kennedy with Haselock provide a fully worked out order of service outline as a stand-alone service. This example was used by a parish in One World Week. The Eucharistic example in NPW is also signposted (Kennedy with Haselock, p. 152–3). Imaginative and creative ideas for interactive and all-age worship are readily available online.

The important thing to note is that none of these suggestions are mandatory and local communities ought to feel free to disregard them. Having said that, it is in rural parishes, as our ecclesiological discussion has highlighted, that these themes around the natural world, justice, cooperation and collaboration with the divine, stewardship, sin, suffering and hope, are likely to be very close to the surface anyway, due to the geography and ecology of the community. What the church is encouraging us to do is to just be a little bit more deliberate about the way in which we plan and organize our worship during this early autumn period. Perhaps the use of the analysis matrix described earlier might aid in gathering, sifting and organizing the material into a coherent season.

The summer and open-air worship

Rediscovering the outdoors

The coronavirus pandemic of 2020–21 has accelerated the rediscovery of the open air as an environment naturally suited to prayer and worship. Although some communities may have been worshipping in the open air very regularly before Lent 2020, the sudden, enforced and prolonged exodus from our church buildings resulted in rapid rethinking of patterns and forms of worship. In the first three months of the first national lockdown all gatherings of any kind for corporate worship were prohibited, other than those of existing households. Clergy were also prohibited from entering the church buildings alone and so alternative venues needed to be sought. Coupled with the permission given by the UK government for individuals or households to exercise outdoors, and an unusually warm and balmy spring and early summer, Christians naturally began to pray in the open air regularly. Pre-recorded and live-streamed worship from vicarage gardens, with readings and intercessions being offered by members of the congregation from their own backyards or front doorsteps, resulted in acts of worship which were highly unusual, creative by necessity, and in many cases deeply moving. Some occasions even made the national consciousness: perhaps the most famous being the Dean of Canterbury, seated on a garden chair with a pot of tea on the table beside him, steadfastly continuing with his morning reflection while his cat strolled nonchalantly into the folds of his cassock!

The first national lockdown of 2020 encompassed the second half of Lent, all of Eastertide, and the Day of Pentecost. Symbolic representations of the stages of the journey of Holy Week appeared in many churchyards, and the Exultet was sung from gardens and deserted churchyards across the land. I personally sang the Exultet from the patio doors of my dining room in Salisbury, streaming live to a congregation from the parishes of Tidenham gathered over Zoom. I also conducted a renewal of baptismal vows from the garden.

The author conducts the renewal of baptismal vows
from his garden, Easter 2020

As restrictions eased in July 2020, worship in church buildings gradually recommenced but very many congregations, including Tidenham, began to include regular open-air worship in their programme, partly out of a wariness about a second lockdown, partly to provide a safer venue for worship than the insides of church buildings were perceived to be and partly because some important learning had been done in those early months. The sharing of worship in a Lent and Easter in virtual confinement to our own homes gave rise to a renewed attention to the natural environment. The reduction in traffic sounds in many places allowed birdsong to break back into our consciousnesses. Taking the hour of permitted exercise each day in our local community allowed us to notice buds growing on the trees and bushes. Reciting the daily Offices in the garden, or next to a window at home, rather than in church during Holy Week and Easter strengthened the implicit connections between the narrative of the Resurrection and the blossoming into life of the natural world:

> Now the green blade riseth from the buried grain,
> wheat that in dark earth many days has laid;
> love lives again, that with the dead has been:
> *love is come again,*
> *like wheat that springeth green.*
> (J. M. C. Crum, New English Hymnal, 115)

In some communities, the Benedicite Omnia Opera, set as an option for use on any day of the year in the BCP Morning Prayer service, tends to be particularly favoured during Lent. With its unfolding vision of the entirety of creation praising God, its words were never more apposite than during Lent 2020:

> O ye Mountains and Hills, bless ye the Lord: praise him,
>   and magnify him forever.
> O all ye Green Things upon the earth, bless ye the Lord:
>   praise him, and magnify him forever.
> (BCP, Morning Prayer)

There would seem to be some strands of useful learning emerging from the experience of 2020.

Moving regular services outdoors

Many parishes have moved some or all their regular schedule of services out of church buildings. Initially this often looked like the minister in his or her garden saying morning or evening prayer, or celebrating the Sunday Eucharist with a camera lens pointing at them. Over the summer, churchyards were utilized by some churches, either to avoid the potential risks to public health of meeting inside a building, or out of a newfound joy in being in the open air. Several parishes over the Christmas of 2020 held their Christmas Eucharist or Crib Service outside in order to permit congregational singing of carols. One strand to reflect on therefore is whether, in the future, more of our regular pattern of worship might appropriately take place out of doors.

TFC provides a fully worked out order of service for a Eucharist during Creationtide and actively encourages the ministers to consider holding it in the open air:

> This Eucharist may be celebrated in the usual place of worship. Local churches are encouraged to consider arranging to have the celebration outside, either in a rural setting, or in a green space in an urban environment, according to the context of the local church. (TFC, p. 49)

At the time of writing this chapter, in January 2021, general permission seems to have been given by the Church of England for Canon B40 to be eased in order to allow Holy Communion to be celebrated routinely elsewhere than in consecrated buildings. This facilitated the celebration of the Eucharist at home during the first lockdown but also permits open-air celebrations in places like churchyards on a regular basis. It will be interesting to see whether, when the Church of England emerges from the immediate stresses of the pandemic, some attention is given to whether the regulations controlling where Holy Communion might be celebrated might be eased on a more permanent basis. This would allow, for example, the Sunday Eucharist to be celebrated in the churchyard when circumstances suggest that might be appropriate. TFC appears to take it as read that it is reasonable to celebrate Holy Communion 'outside, either in a rural setting, or in a green space in an urban environment', and doesn't refer to any permissions needing to be sought. I wonder whether a pattern might emerge in some places where the principal Eucharist of the Sunday is celebrated in the open air in the churchyard once a month during the summer season?

The order of service provided in TFC suggests using the 'Lament for a time of global environmental and climate crisis' as part of the Liturgy of the Word at this open-air Eucharist. It also suggests the use of Eucharistic Prayer G, and this is the one printed in the text of the service. There are sound reasons for this, not least the imagery used in the preface recalling that, 'from the beginning you have created all things and all your works echo the silent music of your praise. In the fullness of time you made us in your image, the crown of all creation' (TFC, p. 55). The drawback with using Prayer G (or indeed any of the 'Eastern' shaped prayers) is that the rather lovely extended prefaces for the agricultural year cannot be used. A local church could, of course, opt to drop in a different eucharistic prayer and use one of the prefaces in CW: TS. The order of service in TFC concludes with the Act of Commitment also discussed above. Although TFC implies that this Eucharist is designed for use during Creationtide it would work equally well on the Second Sunday before Lent or indeed on any summer Sunday where it was desired to make the natural world a particular focus.

There is considerably less canonical restriction on the conduct of non-Eucharistic worship elsewhere than the church building, and so there is great scope for Services of the Word, or morning and evening prayer to be conducted in the open air.

Additional and alternative services during the summer season

In the Severnside Benefice, particularly at Deerhurst, there was a notable increase in worshippers and visitors over the summer due to the proximity of holiday cottages and campsites. The natural buoyancy of mood during the summertime, combined with implicit permission to do different and unusual things, makes it the perfect time to explore using the open air more, speaking to the ecological and environmental themes we have discussed, and perhaps also to address some of the ecclesiological challenges of multi-parochial benefices.

A long-standing tradition in the Parish of Tidenham is the annual pilgrimage to the ruined church of St James the Great, Lancaut (see Figure 1, p. xxv). Since this church was closed in 1865 and allowed to fall into ruins following the removal of the roof that same year, there have been periodic pilgrimages to the site (Clammer and Underwood, pp. 24–5). The tradition was revived in the 1990s, and then re-energized in the last decade. An informal open-air act of worship is held within the ruins of the building on a Sunday afternoon close to the Feast of St James (25 July). Access to the site is via a winding woodland descent, although vehicular access is provided by one of the local farmers for the infirm.

The congregation after open-air worship at
Lancaut church, summer 2019

Lancaut church in the Parish of Tidenham

This service is always very well attended, with significant numbers of elderly and infirm people availing themselves of the bracing ride across the fields to join younger people and families. It works well for a number of reasons: first of all, it is unusual. Doing something once a year, and particularly during the summer, lends a sense of festival to it. Second, the location is idyllic. Worshipping in the open air does something interesting and different to the person praying, as we have reflected above. It is hard to quantify but there is something about the groundedness of praying with no roof between us and the heavens which reminds us of some of those important truths about the relationship between God and his creation. Singing sounds different in the open air and so does speech. Third, there are lots of unusual things for the community to do. People are keen to be asked to help, and to be asked to help to do something like drive your Land Rover to a ruined church is both interesting and exciting. So is stewarding an open-air service, or playing your flute to sustain the singing. Fourth, and this is perhaps the more important ecclesiastical point, the act of worship takes place away from all the currently licensed and consecrated buildings. There is nothing 'party' about this service because it is happening within the parish but away from the regular worship centres. In the case of Tidenham, there is the added blessing that the service takes place within the ruins of a church building, making connections with worshipping communities of the past and bringing to the fore all the themes of eternity and temporality. Many parishes have sites of earlier Christian worship within them, whether they be ruined or entirely vanished churches, preaching crosses, or otherwise. These can be the beginnings of thinking around day pilgrimages. Alternatively, farmyards, school playing fields and village greens provide an ideal location for connecting with the natural environment, and offer a similarly useful 'neutral venue' to which members of all the scattered congregations can be invited. Such services, in addition to being excellent social events, provide the opportunity to cement the identity of a collection of parishes, or united benefice. Telling the stories of the geography and ecclesiology of the local community roots us in where we have come from, and reminds us of the importance of that storytelling tradition. On occasion, at St James's Church, I have preached about which stories future generations might tell about the parish, and alluded to that deeper sense of remembering which is at the heart of so much of our liturgy and common life.

Thorpe reflects on open-air worship thus:

Coming outside can allow for more flexibility and freedom to do new things. It can also help us to reconnect with the experience of the early disciples. Jesus did most of his ministry outside, in the marketplace, beside the lake or in the wilderness. In a time when far fewer people come to church and the culture of church services can be unfamiliar and off-putting, it can help for us to take church outside the four walls of the building and to recapture some of the simplicity and freedom that comes from being in the open-air. (p. 145)

While I would counsel against creating too much of a dichotomy between worship in a traditional building and worship elsewhere, Thorpe is undoubtedly identifying some important missional aspects here. Worship is, of course, always worship wherever we do it, but as we have explored throughout this book there is something significant about context, and greater truths can rise up before us when we worship in a way that enables us to think again, or harder, or differently, about the God to whom all that worship is oriented.

Thorpe's *Ploughshares* offers two interesting services for the summer season. The first one, 'Hedgerow Abundance' is an imaginative take on a flower festival using jam jars of flowers, making it perfect for use in any environment and ideal for use with a local school or summer club (p. 106–12). He also provides an intriguing suggestion of a service focusing on the gift of water and rain (pp. 115–23). With sufficient preparation both services could be waiting in the wings so if an open-air service over the summer is unexpectedly rained off, perhaps the congregation could retreat into a building and use the rain service instead!

I commend the idea of exploring the geography of your local community. Where are the historic sites? Where are the places that have been important in the past? And how do they connect with the present, and speak promise to the future? Can these places become points of pilgrimage? Can they become part of the ongoing formation of the life of the people of God where you are?

As I have already mentioned, just at the point of writing there is a considerable amount of work being done on open-air worship, largely arising from the experience of the coronavirus pandemic, and it will be important to feed those pieces of learning into this conversation. Open-air worship in 2020–21 has occurred over a much wider period than the traditional summer season with experiments being made in winter open-air services. In Tidenham the Christmas Eve 'Bobble Hats and Lanterns' service in the churchyard at Tutshill provided one of the only opportunities in the entire Christmas cycle for congregational carol singing.

Churchyards as oratories

The final thought really builds on the conversations we had around the days after Christmas and Easter, and the ways in which we can help inquirers to encounter the deep mysteries and truths of God even when there is no activity going on in our churches. Some churches are very good at providing a welcome to passers-by, pilgrims, those who are having a constitutional after an excellent pub lunch on a Saturday, or whoever else might pop their heads into the building. Whenever I explore a church and find there are prayer cards, opportunities to light a candle, or that a movement sensor turns on the lights automatically for a period, I instinctively feel welcomed and as if the meagre and muddled prayers I might offer in that building are valued and important to the community. The pandemic has forced us out of our buildings and into our churchyards, and over the great cycles of Christmas and Easter there have been renewed attempts to provide the possibility for such encounter outside. There may be things we could learn from the experience of the pandemic and translate to the everyday. I wonder whether we could turn our churchyards into oratories?

For the rural church, more often than not surrounded by green space, we sit in a natural pool of prayer. I often wonder what prayers are being said when I notice a family laying a bunch of flowers at the place of a burial of ashes, or an elderly person meticulously clipping and tidying a grave of someone buried two generations ago. I really have no idea what they may be saying, thinking or praying, but I am absolutely certain there are valid, hallowed and important connections taking place. Our churchyards, like our church buildings, tell the story of who we are. They connect us to our past, and our presence in them today has things to say about our future. Every prayer offered is another seed in holy ground. I think at this point what I am inviting is a conversation about how we might make it even easier for anyone who stumbles across our rural churches to plant another seed in the fertile soil of God's vineyard. It might be as simple as thinking about having some prayer material available at the lych gate as well as inside the building. It might be about the seasonal use of some prayer stations. It might be thinking a little bit harder about access, lighting and signage. For certain it has to do with welcome, but it has to do with more than that. It has to do with, in the words of the hymn, telling 'the tale of him who brought us out of darkness into light' (C. A. Alington, New English Hymnal, 477).

Joining the threads

The agricultural cycle offers another layer of insight to the rural church community, allowing some of the ecclesiological and theological truths we have considered in relation to Christmas and Easter to be further embedded in our practice. Rather than being a discrete period of the liturgical calendar, the cycle of the seasons of the farming year penetrate and complement the cycle of Sundays and Saints days. The distinctive nature of the rural community offers opportunities to proclaim the great and wonderful truths of our doctrine, revealed through our liturgy, and our rural churches as seeds in holy ground can sing those truths profoundly.

We have considered the specific festivals: Plough Sunday, Rogationtide, Lammastide and Harvest, but we can also recognize those individual occasions as specific examples of something more general about an aspect of doctrine and ecclesiology upon which the Church of England has renewed its focus in recent years. Whether we choose to enhance our observation of the period just before Lent, or develop an autumn 'Creationtide', or both, we find an ever-increasing selection of resources to aid us in our ministry. We have recognized the call upon us to ensure that even when our focus is specifically upon creation and its conservation, we must remember that above all our worship is Christological, that it is in the person of Christ we find the ultimate renewal and sanctification of a creation groaning in travail, and that when we hear creation singing, those songs are praise to Christ.

Energized by the necessary rediscovery of the open spaces

around us, we recognize the promise and potential in worship outside our local buildings. We are inspired to dig into the Christian history of our own environments, discovering where the story of salvation has been told in the past and finding our place in that ongoing adventure of proclamation. We also recognize that, once again, the provision is generous and we will need to be discerning and selective in its use in order to avoid liturgical indigestion. The multi-parochial benefice has the opportunity of using pilgrimage, procession and an exploration of the historical and geographical nature of the parishes to use some of the material available as an opportunity to develop and cement a wider identity, while fulfilling our primary calling to worship the Lord.

6

Crowning the Year: Conclusions

Eternal God,
you crown the year with your goodness
and you give us the fruits of the earth in their season:
grant that we may use them to your glory,
for the relief of those in need and for our own well-being;
through Jesus Christ our Lord. Amen. (CW, p. 447)

In concluding, we return to the Collect for Harvest Thanksgiving. It is a fine prayer and encapsulates a good deal of what
we have discussed. We address our Eternal God, remembering
that above all else the call upon each of our hearts is to praise
God who is eternal, everlasting and faithful love. This is the
first and primary duty and joy of any Christian individual or
community, and as such demands our attention and our care.

Liturgy is the public and corporate worship of the church,
and it tells the story of God's love. Through what we say, sing,
pray and do together we receive the precious deposit of faith,
reflect on it, allow it to form us, challenge us and inspire us,
and then hand it on. The rural Church of England does its
praying in a particular context which forms a distinctive ecclesiology. The coming together of a congregation of Christians
in a particular place, at a particular time, with distinctive and
local hopes, fears, dreams and questions, forms a context in
which the unchanging and unshakeable promises of God are
spoken, received, and proclaimed. That coming together is, in
itself, liturgical theology. Wherever we pray together, reaching
out from our temporal and transient humanity to encounter
eternal faithfulness, theology happens, liturgy happens, transformation happens, and the Church prays.

None of what I have written in the last paragraph is fresh revelation. We have always understood liturgy as both contextual and eternal. That is why the church sets bounds on flexibility, but encourages innovation within those bounds. Two particular places where I hope this discussion might prove useful, however, have to do with more recent developments in the Church of England.

The first of those developments is the burgeoning and blossoming of liturgical material since the end of the twentieth century. We are now faced with enormous variety, and that brings both joys and challenges. Hopefully, what I have suggested here provides a framework of ecclesiology and liturgical theology which, together with a suggested method of 'doing' that ecclesiology and theology in a real parish context, will enable worship leaders and ministers confidently to take up the liturgical resources, relish them, sift them, and make them work in the countryside. In particular, the great seasons of Christmas, Easter, and the agricultural cycle offer such potential for our buildings and our souls to thrill with praise, yet most of the broadly modern catholic liturgical material doesn't speak directly to the rural context. Perhaps some of that deficit has been redressed here.

Second, over the course of our exploration I have offered some places of potential inspiration for a scattered rural community which might be feeling keenly the pressures of falling attendance, reducing clergy numbers and the pressures of buildings and finance. In particular I have suggested that the time-hallowed model of prayer of a religious community has particular things to say to the rural church. Praying absolutely makes a difference. Too often we see it as a soft point in our diary, and it becomes squeezed. When we squeeze prayer, we choke off our own lifeline. Taking up again a pattern of simple, quiet, regular and above all faithful prayer, hour by hour, day by day, season by season is not a new idea. It is nothing less than St Benedict suggested a millennium and a half ago, and he of course found his inspiration in the Scriptures. It has often been said that small churches are *not* failed big churches, and I urge Christians in the countryside to take that seriously. There is a distinctive ecclesiology in the rural Church of England, which looks a bit like a religious community. I believe it is possible the rural Christian community might be being called to a particular ministry of undergirding the world and the church in that sort of prayer. Like individual monks and nuns whispering their prayers in their cells around a cloister, so may a great offering of prayer well up from these tiny seeds in holy ground. That prayer doesn't need to be complicated, showy or grand. It just needs to be there. It just needs to be constant. It just needs to be faithful. That distinctive ecclesiology leads us to use and utilize our liturgy in a particular way, joining our hearts and hands and minds and voices with the rest of the church in common worship and common prayer.

I notice I wrote the first words of this book on Trinity Sunday 2020, with the Church of England in lockdown. I am writing these final words on the Feast of Candlemas 2021. Very many churches have closed their doors to corporate prayer again in the past month, amidst a rising tide of infection and a genuine national emergency. What has struck me over the past year has been quite how resilient prayer is. Whether offered privately, over social media or videoconferencing platforms, in church-yards and gardens and back in our buildings when permitted, 'the voice of prayer is never silent, nor dies the strain of praise away' (J. Ellerton, NEH 252). We have been reminded that we can always talk to God. We have been reminded that, in the end, this is all we must do, and when we do talk to God, all sorts of other things happen. As we, pray God, move into a new chapter in the life of the Church of England, and in par-ticular its rural congregations, may we never again forget that.

> Living stones, by God appointed
> each to his allotted place,
> Kings and priests, by God anointed,
> shall you not declare his grace?
> Ye, a royal generation,
> tell the tidings of your birth,
> tidings of a new creation
> to an old and weary earth (C. A. Alington, NEH 477)

Bibliography

A Time for Creation: Liturgical Resources for Creation and the Environment, 2020, London: Church House Publishing.

Bradshaw, P. (ed.), 2001, *A Companion to Common Worship: volume 1*, London: SPCK.

Clammer, C. and Underwood, K. (eds), 2014, *The Churches and Chapels of the Parish of Tidenham: their history and architecture*, Tidenham: Tidenham Historical Group.

The Canons of the Church of England, seventh edition, 2019, www.churchofengland.org/more/policy-and-thinking/canons-church-england, accessed 1.10.20.

Common Worship: Daily Prayer, 2005, London: Church House Publishing.

Common Worship: Lectionary: Advent 2019 to the eve of Advent 2020, London: Church House Publishing.

Common Worship: New Patterns for Worship, 2002, London: Church House Publishing.

Common Worship: Ordination Services (Study Edition), 2007, London: Church House Publishing.

Common Worship: Pastoral Services, 2nd edition, 2005, London: Church House Publishing.

Common Worship: Services and Prayers for the Church of England, 2000, London: Church House Publishing.

Common Worship: Times and Seasons, 2006, London: Church House Publishing.

Dickens, C., 2018, *A Christmas Carol*, Ware: Wordsworth Editions Ltd.

Dow, G., 2015, *Leading Rural Churches for Growth*, Cambridge: Grove Books (Leadership booklet 19).

Elliott, P., 2002, *Ceremonies of the Liturgical Year According to the Modern Roman Rite*, San Francisco: Ignatius Press.

Gaze, S., 2006, *Mission-shaped and Rural*, London: Church House Publishing.

Gordon-Taylor, B. and Jones, S., 2009, *Celebrating Christ's Appearing: Ash Wednesday to Trinity*, London: SPCK.

Gordon-Taylor, B. and Jones, S., 2009, *Celebrating Christ's Victory: Ash Wednesday to Trinity*, London: SPCK.

GS Misc 803, 2005, *Seeds in Holy Ground: A Workbook for Rural Churches*, London: Acora Publishing.

Herbert, J., 2003, *A Priest to the Temple, or A Country Parson, with Selected Poems*, Norwich: Canterbury Press.

Hobbs, K., 2011, *Growing Churches through House for Duty Ministry*, Cambridge: Grove Books (Evangelism booklet 94).

Hunwicke, J. (ed.), 2020, *Order for the Eucharist and for Morning and Evening Prayer in the Church of England*, Birmingham: Additional Curates Society.

Jones, C. and Martin, J., 2015, *Honey & Thistles: Biblical Wisdom for the Renewal of Farming*, Northampton: Agriculture and Theology Project.

Julian of Norwich, *Revelations of Divine Love (Modern English Translation)*, Kindle Edition.

Kennedy, D. (ed.), 2006, *Using Common Worship: Times and Seasons, All Saints to Candlemas*, London: Church House Publishing.

Kennedy, D., with Haselock, J. (eds.), 2008, *Using Common Worship: Times and Seasons, Lent to Embertide*, London: Church House Publishing.

Kramer, M. J., 'What are we waiting for? Approaching Advent theology through music', *Church Music Quarterly* (December 2020), pp. 30–3.

Lack, P., 2008, *All Mud and Matins? Understanding Rural Worship*, Cambridge: Grove Books (Worship booklet 196).

Lent, Holy Week and Easter: Services and Prayers, 1984, London: Church House Publishing.

Martin, S., with Hewlett, C., Orme, R. and Payne, B., 2015, *Resourcing Rural Ministry: Practical Insights for Mission*, Abingdon: Bible Reading Fellowship.

Merton, T., 1949, *The Waters of Siloe*, New York: Harcourt, Brace and Company.

The New English Hymnal, 1986, Norwich: Canterbury Press.

Perham, M., 2000, *New Handbook of Pastoral Liturgy*, London: SPCK.

The Promise of His Glory: for the Season from All Saints to Candlemas, 1991, London: Church House Publishing.

Thorpe, C., 2020, *Ploughshares and Firstfruits: A Year of Festivals for the Rural Church*, Norwich: Canterbury Press.

Recommended Further Reading

The Daily Office

Fletcher, J. and Myers, G., 2002, *Using Common Worship: Daily Prayer*, London: SPCK.
Does exactly what it says on the tin! Really useful, practical tips together with some theological background.

Guiver, G., 2001, *Company of Voices: Daily Prayer and the People of God*, Norwich: Canterbury Press (second edition).
A scholarly examination of the history and theology of daily prayer by a monk of the Benedictine tradition.

Rural ecclesiology

Francis, L., and Martineau, J., 1996, *Rural Praise*, Leominster: Gracewing.

Sources of devotional liturgical material for Christmas

The Divine Office: The Liturgy of the Hours According to the Roman Rite. Volume 1. Daily Prayer for Advent, Christmastide and Weeks 1–9, 1974, Dublin: HarperCollins.
The Roman Catholic daily Office provides devotional and patristic readings for every day within the 'Office of Readings' section, as well as a selection of seasonal hymns (pp. 547–74) and poetry (pp. 575–79) for which appropriate material could be drawn.

Atwell, R., 1999, *Celebrating the Seasons: Daily Spiritual Readings for the Christian Year*, Norwich: Canterbury Press.
This volume contains a wide variety of devotional material drawn from the patristics all the way through to contemporary theologians and poets, arranged for every day of the liturgical year.

Ambrose, G., Craig-Wild, P., Craven, D. and Hawes, M., 2006, *Together for a Season: All-age Seasonal Resources for Advent, Christmas and Epiphany*, London: Church House Publishing.

Experience Christmas: new edition, Gloucester: Jumping Fish/ Diocese of Gloucester. See www.gloucester.anglican.org/welcome-2/schools/jumping-fish-publications/.
Instructions, ideas and resources for six interactive prayer stations for use in church or school.

Liturgical and devotional material for Holy Week and Easter

Atwell, R., 1999, *Celebrating the Seasons: Daily Spiritual Readings for the Christian Year*, Norwich: Canterbury Press.

The Divine Office: The Liturgy of the Hours According to the Roman Rite. Volume 2. Daily Prayer for Lent and Eastertide, 1974, Dublin: HarperCollins.
The Roman Catholic daily Office provides devotional and patristic readings for every day within the 'Office of Readings' section, as well as a selection of seasonal hymns (p. 569–85) and poetry (p. 607–21) for which appropriate material could be drawn.

Experience Easter: new edition, Gloucester: Jumping Fish/ Diocese of Gloucester. See www.gloucester.anglican.org/welcome-2/schools/jumping-fish-publications/.
Instructions, ideas and resources for six interactive prayer stations for use in church or school. By the same publisher, see also

'Experience Easter Outside', for example of a set of stational resources for the churchyard. Other 'Experience' journeys for the major festivals are also provided.

Ambrose, G., Craig-Wild, P., Craven, D. and Moger, P., 2007, *Together for a Season: All-age Seasonal Resources for Advent, Christmas and Epiphany*, London: Church House Publishing.